HEROIC HEART

HEROIC HEART

The Diary and Letters of

KIM MALTHE-BRUUN

1941-1945

edited by his mother,

VIBEKE MALTHE-BRUUN

and translated by Gerry Bothmer

Random House, New York

FIRST PRINTING

Published in New York by Random House Inc., and
simultaneously in Toronto, Canada, by Random House
of Canada, Limited.
Library of Congress Catalog Card Number: 55-5915
Manufactured in the United States of America
By The Haddon Craftsmen, Inc., Scranton, Pa.
Designed by Peter Oldenburg

Contents

KIM'S CHILDHOOD 1

I CAN'T SAY that I was exactly pleased when I found out that I was going to have him. I was very young and not particularly interested in babies. Besides, I was so loaded down with work that I didn't see how I would be able to assume this additional responsibility. But the child was already a reality which had to be reckoned with, and as the days went by, the thought of the little boy who was on the way filled me more and more. I was alone a great deal—sometimes for weeks at a time—and as I wandered around in the Canadian woods, my thoughts kept on coming back to him. I hoped with all my heart that he would be warm-hearted, kind and intelligent. In my thoughts I endowed him with my big nose which I felt would be suitable for a man. I hoped that his spirit would be noble and his body big and strong. These thoughts constantly occupied my mind and at times so intensely that I was convinced I would be able to pour into him all my strength and all my ideals—all that was best in me—while I held back the rest.

When July 7 came around, I knew that I wouldn't have to wait much longer. As the roads at this time were not passable, I didn't dare count on getting to the village in time, and therefore took the train to Edmonton which was our nearest town. It was none too soon, for the next morning, Sunday, July 8, 1923, my son was born, the son who was to mean so much in my life but whom I treated with such youthful nonchalance during the first few years. . . .

At this time we lived in a small blockhouse about a mile from our farm where we were in the process of building a house. Every morning we rode over there on horseback, I with the baby in front of me on the saddle. When the weather was good he would sleep in a haystack most of the day. He thrived, grew tall and thin, and his first black mop was replaced by the golden hair which he kept throughout his childhood. When I look back on this time and recall his eyes as they were, so big and blue, I can't help feeling that already he had been imbued with that great love of nature which later was to be so characteristic of him.

One day when he was only a few months old, I found the basket empty in which I had left him. Fortunately only a few seconds elapsed before I heard a faint whining from the wheatfields. There he was, a bit frightened, but otherwise unharmed. One of our big greyhounds, wanting to play with him, had dragged him out of the basket and onto the veranda floor, across the stones and out into the fields. . . .

I took him on a visit to Denmark which lasted from December, 1925 to June, 1926; his sister Ruth was born there in February, 1926.

Kim, who until this time had spoken only English, now learned Danish and absorbed many new impressions. . . .

In a letter from Canada dated November 9, 1926, I wrote:

> Kim is as amusing as ever. . . . The other day while we were sitting around chatting, Kim started to sing at the top of his voice. When I asked him to be quiet he said, "Kim isn't singing, but Kim has swallowed a bird—a butterfly—and it is he who keeps on singing." He picks up things quickly, can dry dishes and set a table, all learned by watching.

He wasn't quite three and a half years old then.

It was about this time that a cow of ours, gone completely wild, flew at him, lifted him on her horns and threw him up in the air. His clothes were torn to shreds but he escaped without a scratch.

When he was four he created in his imagination a small family which he called "my people." It consisted of two men, "Pikum" and "Poslum" and a lady who was nameless. Naturally they were the most extraordinary people whose house was filled with cookies, a big red car and horses that were twice as fast as ours. He visited them often, talked to them and waved to them, but when I asked him when we could meet his "people" he always had many good reasons why this wasn't possible. He kept these friends until about the time he started school when other things began to take hold of his fertile imagination.

His school life in Canada was an adventure in itself. In a small wooden shack a young teacher equipped with only the basic minimum of education tried to teach all subjects to about two dozen children, divided into nine groups. It was a long school day and the school was far from where we lived. Kim skied there in winter and in summer he rode on horseback. It was hard going and once when he felt himself dangerously close to frostbite he had to ask for shelter in a farmhouse. But this rugged existence at such an early age hardened him and instilled in him the feeling of belonging to nature which was such a fundamental part of his personality.

His education was negligible, but he did acquire the habit of contemplation and always took great pains to convey to his little sister the result of his deliberations. Once when he was six he said to Ruth, "Jesus already knew everything when he was born: walking, reading and arithmetic," and added with an air of authority, "You mustn't say 'He' about God." The little one nodded gravely and asked, "Should I say 'She'?" She wasn't yet four so he probably had a hard time trying to get across to her what he did mean.

About this time he nearly frightened us to death by falling off a roof and hurting his head badly. His skull was probably fractured, but we didn't notice it at the time, and throughout his life he had a huge, angular scar on his scalp.

When the children were nine and six years old, I took them back to Denmark via New York. For a time we lived with my cousin, Miss Anna Ida Bruun, at Hellerup. From the first day she showed a great interest in Kim, and in spite of the enormous age difference, a warm friendship sprang up between them. The many long discussions with Nitte played an increasingly important role in his life.

It wasn't easy for Kim to adjust himself to the school in Denmark, partly because he was behind the children of his age as far as his education was concerned, and also because he had to cope with the problem of a new language. This school was the fifth in his young life. Small wonder that he failed his high school entrance examination. His ideas on spelling were vague, to put it mildly, and spelling remained one of his weak points for a long time.

Fortunately for Kim, the principal at Stenhus proved to be most understanding. It was here that he spent the next five years of his life. At first he was sixteenth in a class of sixteen but he improved steadily. His first report card, dated October, 1935, read: "Kim is a normally gifted boy but hardly high school material. He has great difficulties in concentrating and his daydreams seem to have the upper hand. His physical development is premature, which may help to explain his lack of energy for mental work." But on the whole his years at Stenhus were happy, although they were for him a time of internal struggle and growing pains. He was fairly happy at school but home to him was much more important. He showed his friends around our house as if he had been displaying the most precious collections at Rosenborg Palace, and his eyes shone with pride and pleasure. But as vacations would draw to a close he became increasingly silent.

His strong desire for freedom didn't fit into the confining atmosphere of boarding school life, but fortunately Stenhus was so free and easy that he never felt oppressed. As far as his school work was concerned he was downright lazy, but got by for several years on his wits, and by giving the impression that he was a hard worker. I think that Kim was in his fourth year at Stenhus when he was found out, because when he came home at the end of the school year he told us that paradoxically enough his marks had never been better, but never had he been scolded more by his teachers. "The principal always thought that I was stupid but that at least I worked hard. Now he has found out that I can work if I want to, but that I've been loafing, and he's mad as a hatter—not because I've been lazy but because he had sized me up all wrong."

After the entry of the Germans into Denmark on April 9, 1940 Kim wrote:

> You can't imagine with what despair we heard the news of what has happened. A feeling of patriotism of which we weren't aware in peacetime has flared up in us. I was in Holbaek the other day when the real German troops arrived. They were riding along, their machine guns over their knees singing "Deutschland, Deutschland über Alles" with all their might. You can't imagine how revolting they were. You could see the Danes who were standing there just boiling. Here at school everything is done to have life go on as usual, but everyone is heavy-hearted. What else could you expect? Today we covered all the cellar windows with boards and sand, and we're going to use the cellar as a shelter. How have you managed the blackout arrangements, and what are your thoughts about the desperate situation Denmark is in? What are the reactions of the people in Copenhagen? It's a gruesome thought, but everything seems to point to a German victory. Here everyone seems to think that if they win we'll be allowed to keep our independence because they want to show that they can be trusted. But no one is going to make me believe that.

During his last year at Stenhus Kim was lazier than ever. It was an extremely cold winter and most of his time was spent ice sailing on the fjord or skiing. He was often out on the fjord until late at night, and it was therefore no surprise when in June, 1940 he was graduated with very bad grades.

As a kind of punishment for his poor scholastic record, he was sent to the country to work as an agricultural trainee, although he couldn't have been less interested in agriculture. But the hard physical labor was definitely what he needed. He became very much interested in the farmers, their problems and their daily life, but the sea held a strange fascination for him. In August he enrolled as a student at the Lauritzen Shipping Company in Svendborg. He remained there until March, 1941 when he was signed on a three-masted schooner as apprentice seaman.

Before Kim went to sea, he spent about a month at home, and it was during this time that he met Hanne. He was immediately aware of the nature of his feeling for her and it wasn't easy for him to leave without telling her his secret. So many months were to go by before they would meet again.

Kim was seventeen when his life as a man and as a seaman began.

Vibeke Malthe-Bruun

Hellerup, Denmark
October, 1945

DANZIG 2

DANZIG

18 May 1941

Dearest Hanne,

I've just arrived here. The weather is marvelous—hardly a breeze, not a cloud in the sky. But it's maddening to see the Germans parading around here. They even come on board.

I'm lying on the big hatch cover as I write this and I'm in a perfect spot to see everything that's going on.

At midnight on Thursday, May 15, my thoughts went out to you, but I was sad because I couldn't be with you on your birthday. But just the same I was with you all that day, Hanne. . . . Rarely have I been so happy and so sad at the same time. As I paced up and down on the lookout for mines, I thought of you and felt warm all over. . . . I could see your mother congratulating you on your birthday and I was there when you opened your presents. I was also around in the afternoon when you had invited a few friends in for a cup of chocolate and I trailed you until you were again in your bed when the day passed in review before your eyes. I hoped so much that you would also be thinking of me. When you had fallen asleep, I kept on watching over you until 4 o'clock the next morning. I was off duty during the next four hours and admit that I slept like a top. You can imagine, my darling, all the plans and thoughts that went through my head during this time—plans and thoughts that I won't go into right now, perhaps later.

We still don't know where we go after we leave here, but as usual I'm hoping that it will be Copenhagen or its vicinity.

I was interrupted. A big German submarine passed us at a distance of not more than twelve feet. It was one of the biggest ones on its way to its mission of destruction on the open seas. You can't imagine the horror of seeing one of those "coffins" and all the anguish of the women and children crying as they run along the quay. The Germans themselves are the cause of all this misery, but it's a terrible thing to see just the same.

Sweetheart, here I am again. I went ashore to look around. The destruction is unbelievable: shell holes everywhere and trees stripped of their bark and ruined. In the woods about three minutes' walk from here is a small barracks completely shot to pieces. The bullet holes aren't even three feet apart. The battle of Poland was a catastrophe and what an unspeakable horror that the Germans should be the victors! Around here we almost go out of our minds at the thought of the Germans—in fact, everything German. When I see how they treat their prisoners of war, I could slit their throats, every last one of them.

This place, as well as Stettin, has an aviation school and as a result the sky is filled with all sorts of planes. They certainly manage to look impressive, but we curse them because they are German and keep hoping that they'll crash, which unfortunately hasn't happened until now—at least not while we were watching.

Tomorrow I have watch, but I still have to work with the others, so I'll probably be dead by tomorrow night. It's amazing how little sleep I can get along on when necessary. Several times we've worked around the clock without being too knocked out. But when I finally do bunk down, I sleep like a log and am not too pleased at having to get up again after a few hours. Hanne, do you know that when I lie down I dream wonderfully about you until I fall asleep? It's like the times when I have watch on a clear moonlit night—I feel as if I could fly and my dreams take off on such flights of fancy that it would be impossible to hold onto them in full daylight. How I wish that you could live through a night like this with me at sea! Then you would understand what I mean.

DANZIG
19 May 1941

Hello, my darling. I'm just about dead, but I still want to write a few words to you. Today we were told that we're going to Vejle, which was an awful disappointment to me. My shipmates are thrilled to pieces because rumor has it that the girls there are very pretty. But what does that matter to me when my girl doesn't live in Vejle? From there we will probably go on to Aabo, Finland. It will be a great relief to get out of Germany, which is rotten to the core, although it will be terrible to be away from you for so long. But this will only make me twice as happy to see you when I do come home.

Tonight I had a stroke of bad luck. I was visiting a Danish ship which is anchored right in front of us, and when I jumped from the ladder onto their deck cabin I didn't notice a hook lying there with the pointed end up. It went right through my rubber shoe and into my foot. It was a thick one and made a nasty wound. It's going to be hard work standing up tomorrow, but I hope I'll manage. The first mate cleaned the wound and pressed out as much dirt as he could, so here's hoping that it will heal without becoming infected.

You should have seen what we saw this morning—a big cart loaded with stone to which Polish prisoners were harnessed! Behind them came two Germans with bayonets. We were all beside ourselves with fury and disgust at the display of such brutality, and at that moment I could have murdered any German. This made me think of how the Danish peasants used to behave in times past and I asked myself what sort of progress in human behavior we have to show in the year 1941.

DANZIG
20 May 1941

Copenhagen-Kalundborg, Hanne, Kim calling—the best connection anyone has ever had. I hardly slept a wink last night because of the damned leg, but this gave me all the more time to think—of course not about you at all! But I'm sure you won't believe that. It hurt like all blazes and lying still in bed made me all the more aware of it. The pain was caused by a piece of rust which the first mate hadn't gotten out last night. He managed to get it out today with a knife and by applying a bit of elbow grease. After he had opened it up, it felt much better in spite of the stinging and burning. I hope you don't think I'm writing all this in order to play on your sympathy, because I'm not. It was my own fault—I should have watched my step. But I'm writing this because it helps me get over this kind of minor irritation if I can share it with you.

As I sit here soaking my leg in a hot soap solution, I'm reading this through. I feel like tearing it up right away, but Hanne, if I throw it in the fire, you won't hear from me at all. I must feel that I can write you no matter under what circumstances—filthy, exhausted, in any mood, and no matter how awful the results are. If I were at home and didn't have to do all this hard physical work, I would be able to write you amusing and newsy letters, but I don't think they would be quite as sincere, or that I would be as honest with myself as I am now. I hope that you will accept them as they are. Perhaps they may even improve when I get accustomed to this life. I want so very much to make an impression on you, but I can't. I know it and now I can only hope and pray that you will understand and forgive me.

And now I'm about to hit the sack. Good night, my love.

DANZIG
21 May 1941

Here I am—in bed. When I woke up this morning, my leg was swollen and sore as the devil, and when the skipper saw it he immediately whisked me away to a doctor who told me it was a bad case of blood poisoning. He told the skipper that the leg, the foot, and perhaps even my life was in danger. He threw up his arms in despair and glanced at me to see if I had understood what he was saying. He wanted to take me to a hospital and the skipper was all for it, since he felt that he couldn't take the responsibility for me. I put in violent objections for two reasons. First of all, I couldn't think of a worse fate than being left behind in a German hospital, and my second reason was that I had no desire to sign off the ship now that I was earning a good wage and working together with some decent fellows. I knew that I would be sorry for the rest of my life if I stayed behind. Besides, I don't quite trust that doctor. He's just a little bit too eager to get me into the hospital. I admit that my leg looks pretty awful, but I refuse to believe that it is as bad as he would have me think.

As you can well imagine, I was in pretty bad shape going to and from the doctor's. My foot was so swollen that I couldn't get a shoe on, so I had to wrap it in a burlap bag—very fancy-looking. People in the street turned around and stared. Believe me, it was the longest walk I ever took. The trip back was especially bad, since the foot hurt twice as much after it had been opened. When I got back on board I was ordered to go to bed, and the skipper came and gave me a compress hotter than blazes. As you can imagine, it hurts like hell and now I'm trying to drive away all the bad thoughts by writing to you. I'm lying in such an awkward position that writing is damned difficult. My hands and arms are all pins and needles, but I think that I could write to you no matter what.

It's hopeless even to think of getting home for Whitsun, since our coal still hasn't arrived and it's reported that the railroad by which it was to come was bombed last night.

On my way from the doctor's I passed a whole gang of Polish laborers who worked in a gravel pit at the side of the road, guarded by a fat German. One of the Poles who was standing at some distance from the others made a sign asking for a cigarette. As it happened, I had my whole allowance of two hundred on me. He was as grateful as if I had put the riches of the world in his lap. I made a sign to indicate that he should share them with the others. When I see them having to work like beasts for the Germans, I would gladly give them anything I own. Unfortunately, it's no use since the Germans confiscate anything worth taking—the damned swine.

You should have seen some of the miserable creatures sitting in the doctor's waiting room, thin, haggard and harassed, and every time someone walked into the room his greeting was "Heil Hitler." An old Polish woman came into the drugstore. "Heil Hitler" was the first thing she said, although she damns him from the bottom of her heart. But everyone is forced to do it. Even the prisoners of war have to salute their guards and tyrants with "Heil Hitler." My mate here says that Hitler is the devil's lightning rod on earth.

You know, I wish so very much that you would write me everything that interests you—little things which have amused you and caught your fancy. This will help me to follow you on the wings of my imagination and be with you in between times when I have a free moment to dream about you.

DANZIG
22 May 1941

Hello, hello, where are you? I'm trying to establish connections. I think the doctor was right after all—I'm sick all right. He came yesterday to have a look at my leg. My fever was up to 101. The leg had turned an ugly color with dark blue stripes. They have been changing the dressing every hour during the last twenty-four hours. If there were only some sign of improvement! But it seems as if it's steadily getting worse. There were times last night when I almost felt that I should have listened to the doctor yesterday. I spent the night cursing my fate, being happy at the thought of you and mulling over world problems in general.

I couldn't help thinking about what queer creatures we all are. This is something to ask yourself—and to answer: what is the foundation on which you plan to build your life? Have you ever thought about it seriously? Some people can't seem to find the answer to this and instead abandon themselves to a religion of some kind in order to fill the gap which would otherwise exist in their lives. Most people bypass the question as being too thorny to tackle, but if they do, they don't count with us.

Just think how wonderful it would be if more of us would make honesty the basic principle of our lives—how very much that word implies! If only we would be honest with ourselves, how much happier we would be and how rewarding life itself would be! Isn't honesty the most important single course to follow? Is there a truth or a fact which could be developed if this concept were unknown? Love, for instance; what is love but honest and true feelings—it is to me, in any case.

If we only fully realized that each time we tell a lie, whether intentional or not, we pick a small stone out of the foundation upon which our life is built. For the same reason the relationship between man and woman can't possibly be harmonious if both parties don't have complete faith in each other, if they don't feel deep down that every emotion of the other is honest and not something which has only come to the surface as a result of a mood or an impulse. What will be the fate of societies which build their whole future on one lie after another, and what right to existence do they have if they don't know what honesty means? How can anyone who doesn't live according to the principles of truth be in a position to judge others? We all find it much too easy to condemn our fellow man for his sins and to overlook our own. I have often been disgusted with people—myself included—who are quick to condemn a man with all the righteous indignation so typical of us when we are judging others. How can we keep on living in this insincere way, covering up everything with lies and only knowing the word truth by name? How does this enable us to judge what is right and what is wrong? He who collects evidence to condemn another only brings it upon himself in eternity.

It isn't truth which involves and complicates life; on the contrary, it simplifies and makes clear the road ahead. Love is a form of truth. It makes everything so easy and natural. But lies complicate everything and destroy from beneath what is noble and beautiful. They force their way in and slowly but surely tear down all that truth and love have built; they pick away the small stones from the foundation of the structure which was perfect and whole.

So many feel that adhering to principles is a boring, unadventurous sort of life, but the same people have the same ideas about love—that it is much too complicated and that life should be gay and without entangling alliances. If they only knew how much they were missing! Love is the most precious and beautiful of all things that life has to offer. What a narrow-minded and cowardly stand to take—not daring to face the truth squarely—not daring and not wanting to bother with the little cares which are in the path of everything beautiful and worthwhile. They are blind to the fact that these obstacles double the value and beauty of life. How much these little moments of anguish add to the wonder of love! How could love and all the marvelous things which make up life be evaluated if there didn't exist a set of values by which to measure them? What would white mean to us if we hadn't seen black?

When I walk on deck on a starlit night and look up at the sky, I feel as if I could suddenly look into eternity, and in a flash I see what an unimportant tiny wheel I am in the great machine of creation. A moment like this also brings into focus the fact that a mere individual is of no importance and doesn't have the right to make demands or compromises. You know how inspiring it is to be together with a noble and brilliant person; you feel so small and unimportant and sit quietly and listen to his thoughts and opinions on all kinds of problems. I hope that you and I will listen in the same reverent way to the greatest teacher of them all—Life itself—and learn anything we can from it.

I seem to have more fever now and am feeling pretty miserable, so I'll have to stop. But it did me so much good to write to you. I hope that you'll be able to read this. I can't do any better in my present condition.

DANZIG
23 May 1941

The crisis came last night. The doctor was here and they kept on feeling my pulse. I was in agony and too exhausted to protest. I think that they opened the wound again and squeezed out all they could. For the first time I felt sorry for myself and cursed my fate. But I sternly asked myself, "Are you or are you not a seaman?" Now I really think I understand what it means to muster all your will power to overcome physical suffering. The doctor told the skipper—probably assuming that I didn't understand German—that it was a question of life and death and that I mustn't be moved. Deep down I wasn't afraid at all. I thought of my mother and felt sorry for her. Then I thought of you, Hanne, and wondered how you would take this last message from me. I kept thinking what a miserable letter this was with nothing but a lot of big words, so completely out of place in my life. It's useless to deny it; I wasn't above taking a certain pleasure in this outpouring—to impress you, of course. I'm not as bad as I sound, but I feel that I ought to make myself tell the truth about myself.

If only I were at home now, I would lie and wait for your footsteps on the stairs. But I'm also happy here because I can keep on writing to you all the time, even though I feel so weak and miserable. Before the doctor left last night, he gave me something to deaden the pain. In my fever I had hallucinations and they were marvelous because we were together.

Have you ever let yourself be carried away on the wings of your imagination? Let's wander off hand in hand, you and I. We are walking through a wonderful pine forest. Oh, if you only knew how much the delicate skin around your little fingernail means to me! I press your hand and you respond; we look into each other's eyes. I see how slowly a smile lights up your eyes. We laugh and wander on, deeply moved by the knowledge that we belong together. Now the road turns to the right and we quicken our steps to see what surprises nature has in store for us this time. A lovely little lake lies before us. What an enchanting spot! We stand absolutely still, deeply affected by the sight of so much beauty gathered in one place. Are you still with me or are you getting weary? We sit down at the water's edge and you chew idly on a straw. How tender, how charming you look! I'm sure that your thoughts are as clear and pure as the spring which flows into the lake over there by the big pine. They are so lovely and so delightfully imaginative that even if I were able to read them I wouldn't be able to grasp their full depth and meaning. Now you're stretched out in the grass with your arms above your head watching a big dragonfly on a branch above you. How you must be marveling at its delicate frame, the webbing of the wings and the wonderful blend of the colors! While you are intently watching it, I in turn am marveling at all the joy and all the beauty which life has given me, and I feel as if I would gladly give all the rest of my life just to be alive this moment. Hanne, do you also feel that love is not only being absorbed in each other, but it is also being able to be absorbed in something together? If it seems to you that this is feverish rambling, I can assure you that I also give way to my imagination when I'm well.

One of the boys just came down to tell me that they are putting up a hammock so that beginning tomorrow I can lie on deck in the sun. I'm so looking forward to getting out into the fresh air again. . . . This is the kind of thoughtfulness which makes me feel that seafaring people are better than most. They are rough and ready in their daily life, but always kind and thoughtful in their own gruff way if you're sick or in trouble.

Something funny is going on here. All Norwegian and Danish ships are being held up under the pretext that there isn't enough coal for fuel while the Russians and Swedish ships are allowed all they need. Our skipper is hopping mad. He's afraid that the Germans are planning to confiscate Danish ships for their own use, but I hope it isn't as bad as all that.

DANZIG
24 May 1941

The doctor just left. He was very satisfied with the patient. Now that the worst is over I'll make a speedy recovery, thanks to the strong physique which in his opinion I'm lucky enough to have. Now I'm looking forward to getting up and working in the sun again. For the first time last night I slept like a top.

While I was lying here in the twilight last night after it had grown too dark to write, I thought about what I had already written you in this letter and what I wanted to write you today. I've forgotten most of it but some of it stuck, and I would like to share with you some of these thoughts from the darkness.

Has it occurred to you how much security and confidence education gives? Countless times since I left school I've been struck by this. If you only knew how mad I am at myself for being so stupid that I didn't take the opportunity of learning something while I had it. There is only one thing which consoles me: I do have the chance to gather knowledge and experience about the subject which is most important of all—people. One of my aims in life is to learn as much about human nature as possible and to profit from it. It's a good beginning, to be able to learn from your own mistakes, but it is still better to be able to profit from the mistakes of others. If we only could develop a society which evaluated its people according to their worth and not according to birth, inheritance or worldly goods.

A man of noble mind is of infinitely more worth than a man of noble birth. If this were instilled in us, we would never be taken in by names, decorations, titles and the like, and the poor man would be equal in stature with the duke. The Germans have adopted a few of these ideas, only to misinterpret them grossly, and are doing the exact opposite. The world shouldn't be controlled the way criminals are—with force and might, but by the self-discipline of each individual. If it were only possible to raise the moral level of a people to the point where they would rise above their own personal desires and work for a higher goal, the same goal which everyone seems to be groping around for but can't seem to see for the smoke of war and all kinds of disturbances. A civilization having this kind of spiritual force and power would be happy beyond anything we can imagine at present.

These are only dreams of the future, but I believe in all the good which is in man and that his development will one day reach the point where he will find greater pleasure in being helpful to others and making them happy than in putting himself first. In the far distant future the spiritual side of man's life will have made so much progress that this ideal will be a reality.

It certainly isn't technical progress which is conflicting with spiritual growth, but I'm sure that thus far it has been our spiritual shortcomings which have held us back.

You should have been here a few minutes ago. Two little fellows, barelegged and with their hair closely cropped the way they all are here, came begging us for a piece of rye bread with lard. Now the children here are beginning to starve—they all look pale and undernourished. How could we feel anything but pity for these kids! What have they done to deserve all this misery? We fed them all they could eat on one condition: that they wouldn't tell anyone. They just went wild, stuffed themselves to the gills and raced home to tell all about their good luck as soon as they had crammed down the last mouthful. Just think of how the parents must feel when the kids come home and tell them that they have been fed on a foreign ship. How awful it must be for them to know that they can't even provide the bare necessities!

There are warships of all sizes in port and more came today. The wildest rumors are going around that a war with Russia is about to break out, and at the moment there are lots of signs pointing in that direction. Let them fight all they want, but oh, if they would only wait until we get out of here!

I probably don't need to tell you that I can't see the lines on the paper any more, so I'll say good night, but I'll continue to be with you in my thoughts. Good night, my darling Hanne.

DANZIG
Sunday, 25 May 1941

Good morning! And how did you sleep last night? Is there anything I can do for Mademoiselle; is she happy and well?

I feel on top of the world this morning, full of life and vigor, having slept soundly! I long so terribly for you. I'm going just crazy lying here, and now that I feel so well I can't reconcile myself to having to stay in this bunk. I'm going to spend all morning in the hammock up on deck and the afternoon, too, I hope. The boys reported that the weather didn't look too good, but I'm hoping they'll turn out to be wrong. It would be more than I could stand to have to lie around here all day—and perhaps several more, and this letter would get to be so long that you wouldn't feel like reading it.

Evening: I've been loafing all day in the sun; my food was brought up. I'm happy to be alive and am my old self again, except for one thing—I'm plagued with bedbugs. They are eating me alive, and my arms and legs are swollen with bites. It's partly due to the heat and maybe also because I spend most of the time in my bunk. It bothers me all the more now because I'm not sick any more. It's just unbearable and I'd give anything to be rid of them. My one consolation is that I have only eighteen months to go on these wooden crates.

Today all of a sudden I felt like playing a game of tennis. I dreamed that we were having a game. You gave some good serves and beat me, although it was close. It was great fun and we'll have to do it again. At the moment the boys are sitting around debating whether to play hide-and-seek, blindman's buff or some other children's games. They are talking excitedly and with lots of enthusiasm. It's all the more astounding to me after having heard them discuss women with profound knowledge backed up by a wealth of experience, which made me a bit uncomfortable in the beginning.

Once more it's twilight, bringing this feeling of being so close to nature and putting me in a confidental mood that makes me want to open up and talk about the things which are closest to my heart. I'm in a mood which is always gone by daylight and which makes me feel like sharing these thoughts with the one person who understands.

I feel so stupid when I read something which I've tried to express on paper. Ordinary and superficial words jump out at me which contain nothing at all of what I was trying to say. I know it's idiotic to attempt the impossible, but Hanne, it would also be impossible for me not to. I just can't help it. Perhaps you find it boring that I keep on pouring out all my feelings to you in this way, but they are what fill my whole existence and give my life a meaning. It would be easy for me to tell you how wonderful you are, but that wouldn't be me and it wouldn't begin to express the feeling in my heart for you. "Heart" is perhaps an expression on its way out, but to me the heart will always be the place from which my deepest feelings come.

Do you know what it's like to sit by a roaring fire and let your mind wander? That is the way I feel at the moment. I'm lying flat on my back—as flat as I can since my bunk is a bit narrow—and staring into the flame of a candle that I've put on the blade of a knife and forced into a crack. When I write,

I hold the pad directly above me with my left hand. My foot is wrapped in a towel which is fastened to the deck beams so that it resembles a sling and keeps the foot up as high as possible. I'm as comfortable as a prince at the moment, but it could be that the prince wouldn't be of the same opinion. Excuse me for a moment while I go on a big-game hunt in the jungle. The wild animals are the bedbugs, the jungle is my bunk and the gun is a lighted candle with which I very slowly (in order to enjoy my revenge) burn them to death.

Hello, I'm back again. The result of the hunt: sixty-seven bedbugs; expenditure of ammunition: eight spots of candle wax on my blanket. This is the best bag I've ever had. I found a crack between the boards of my bunk where they were as numerous as pebbles on the beach. I scraped them out with my knife and, trembling with buck fever, I could hardly wait to get them up in the light. Their screams caused me pangs of conscience which will undoubtedly disturb my peaceful sleep. I hope that you'll be tolerant of my inherited homicidal tendencies.

I'm sorry that I had to cut this short last night but my candle toppled over when I wanted to ask the night watch for some water. Since neither of us had a match, I was forced to postpone the hunt for the time being. Now I'm comfortably installed in the hammock lapping up sun. I feel on top of the world although a bit pooped. Today for the first time I was allowed to maneuver myself up on deck and into the hammock. From down in the cabin I can reach the edge of the trap door with my hands and in this way hoist myself up. Like a little girl playing hopscotch I jumped from there to the hammock.

The weather is once more its pleasant self. I'm having a wonderful time watching four little German boys playing. We're docked along the edge of the canal—practically up on the banks. There are ten to fifteen yards of reeds, after which comes a steep incline of twelve yards or so, and above are the woods. The town is on the other side. The children are playing in the woods and on the incline. They're not exactly handsome with their closely cropped heads, but it's fun watching them. They are much more natural in their games than it would seem at first, and their pranks are as delightful as the movements of a little bird on a limb busily sprucing up or taking a bath. They are so far above the evils of the world, even though they can be forced down to its level in the matter of a few seconds.

Today I got orders to start work again, but since my leg isn't much good for walking as yet and since I'm supposed to keep off it completely, I've been given a job as night watchman. All I have to do is to sit in the galley during the night and keep my eyes and ears open so that no one makes off with anything, and in case of an air raid limp over and put out the lantern. I'm in the galley now. This leg of mine hurts like hell, but I suppose that is to be expected after it's been in a horizontal position for so long. It's probably just as well to get going on it right away and hope that everything will be O.K.

This was the chance I was waiting for, to give myself a good scrubbing—the first in eight days. It was wonderful! Now I'm heating water to wash all my clothes during the night. It's hotter than blazes in here so all I have on is shorts and shoes. You can't imagine what a marvelous feeling it is to be clean again. The next few nights will be long, although I can make them seem much shorter by writing to you.

I'm back again. It's almost 3 A.M. and I've been washing clothes for the past four hours. Not a very amusing job but good to have it over with and to know that I've solved the dirty laundry problem.

I've been thinking that this letter might possibly come as

quite a surprise to you. I've just been going along taking for granted that I mean a lot to you. It's terribly vain of me because I have nothing to offer you except my love and perhaps that doesn't mean too much to you.

The birds have started to sing and the eastern horizon has turned a rosy red. How I wish that you were here and could enjoy the splendor of this hour! A sunrise like this just can't be described in words. So many thoughts are running through my head at this moment, and they all have to do with my greatest desire—to do all in my power to make you as happy as possible. Hanne, should you come home late one night and sit down for a moment to enjoy the moonlight before going inside—think of me. At the same moment I'll be thinking of you. If you thought of me while sitting there, I would feel it and the connection between us would be established.

The wildest rumors are going around here that the Germans have sunk a whole lot of English warships—big ones, that America has officially entered the war and that the Germans are about to attack Russia. The tension is growing by the hour. The Germans have planted a double row of mines outside the port and in here they have gathered together several fleet units. It looks as if we'll be right in the middle of the line of fire when the war against Russia is launched. According to what the German soldiers say, all relations with the Russians are broken off and they are only waiting for the shooting to start. I can't swear to the truth of these rumors because as a matter of principle I don't talk to the Germans except when I try to tell them how stupid and futile their policy is and how little hope there is for them.

I almost forgot the most important thing. Thank you for thinking of me yesterday. I can't tell you what it meant to me that you stayed up and thought of me all night. I hope that the next day wasn't too strenuous for you. I awakened the cook at 6 A.M. He was in a mood for something sweet and made a pudding for us before he went off duty.

My leg is getting better every day, and today I tried to walk on it for the first time. It hurt, but I'm sure that'll be over before long. The doctor looked at it and seemed pleased. I hope to be completely over this by the time we get home.

I'm sure that something will break tonight because there has been a wild buzzing of planes overhead, the like of which I've never seen. This time they seem to have a purpose and are not just playing around as before. Lots of them have left and only a few have arrived. They have been taking off most of the night, one after another, all heading toward the south. If the lid blows off now, it will certainly be interesting to have been on the spot, but "interesting" won't be the word for it if we're still here when the shooting starts.

There goes the first morning twitter of a bird. To me that's a good sign because it means that before long I can put out the lantern and bunk down—and how I'm looking forward to that! So now I'm all through for the night and scrubbed from top to toe like a good little boy.

DANZIG WESTER PLATTE
Wednesday, 28 May 1941

Being anchored here is beginning to get boring. This was not what I had hoped for when we left.

It's midnight. I've just made the rounds to see that everything is in order. I looked up at the stars and thought of you, Hanne, the way you were when we last met. Suddenly it dawned on me how poor my vocabulary is. I can't even convey to you the color of the sky as it was then, the thoughts that were going through my head or even one of the many little moods which make up a night like that. If I were only able to recall it to you exactly as it was, I think that I might be able to win your heart—and there is nothing I want more.

It's kind of strange to see from what different angles people of the different social groups of the community look at just about everything and what a terrifically important role education plays in all of this. Take seafaring people, for example. They look at women from only one angle—the erotic one, and aside from this they are only able to appreciate their capacity for work. I have often seen a seaman with a wife or a sweetheart at home take off with the first floozie he meets when he hits port. These fellows are basically honest and on the whole it doesn't affect the relationships with their loved ones back home. They call a spade a spade, and frankly, once I got used to it, I found something straightforward and honest in this attitude, even though it's not for me.

I asked one of my mates how he would feel if he heard that his wife or sweetheart had behaved the same way. He was surprised and almost horrified that I could even think that he would have anything further to do with such a woman. I asked him how he could expect her to be faithful to him if he wasn't faithful to her. He was as honest as anyone could be. There wasn't an ounce of deceit in him and he loved his wife as sincerely as a man can love. In this case it's only his upbringing which has given him this way of looking at things which seems so odd to us.

Personally, I feel that he, with his simple and straightforward approach, is a cut above the rest of us as far as basic honesty is concerned. When I think of myself and how muddled my thinking is! It's so muddled that quite often I feel as if I'm not even able to be honest with myself and that the real truth escapes me because I've wandered off on the wrong track. Now, for instance, I'm writing you that I'm a spineless good-for-nothing and I really mean it, but still I feel sort of pleased with myself that I can be so "honest" with you. I try to get on the inside track of my thoughts and feelings, but it frightens me because no matter how I turn and twist I can't seem to get hold of the complete truth about myself. Only in one instance have I felt it with a sort of divine clarity, and that is in my love for you. This is the only part of my life about which I know that I'm completely honest and sincere and that I have no mixed feelings.

How I wish that it would be possible for me to reach a state of perfect happiness so that I would also be able to make you happy!

My motto is going to be: "Make truth light the way." I hope that you'll understand what I'm trying to say. Please don't conclude from this that I have an inferiority complex, because I certainly don't, but since I first met you I've been trying to get to know myself and I'm shocked at some of the ideas I used to have about all sorts of things. This makes me realize that I couldn't have found a better way of life than that of a seaman. It gives me the chance I need to think things through and to develop and discipline my character. Despite the general opinion to the contrary, life has taught me that work shouldn't be the aim in life, but a means of forming and developing character. The spiritual and emotional life of man is far more important than material gain. I don't mean that I don't want to amount to anything. On the contrary, the struggle to make something of oneself is also an important part of development. What I mean is that we must make sure that the goal doesn't become so important that it obscures everything else.

I hope that this doesn't sound like a lot of big, empty words to you. But if you understand what I mean, I'm sure that you'll feel the same way I do.

This is breakfast time for me. The sun is about to come up and everything is so beautiful that I could shout with joy. Life at sea to me is as marvelous as a summer vacation is to a little boy. Now it's time for me to put out the lantern and turn to.

DANZIG WESTER PLATTE
Thursday, 29 May 1941

Clouds and rain. Today I went to the doctor to get some salve for my foot because the skin is peeling off. It seems to have had enough of hot compresses and acetic acid. It's one great big blister, but otherwise everything is O.K., thank goodness.

I wish you could see the life on this canal. Perhaps you've read something about it. There are lots of old tenders around that look as if they were about to fall apart any minute. Entire families live on board, including also a dog or a cat. The stern serves as living quarters. The windows, which are small and square and of the same type that you would find on a Danish farm, are decorated with brightly colored curtains and potted plants. There is always a large wash drying on deck. A little boy of about eight in a pair of tattered pants and a still more tattered shirt stands at the rudder. The whole family takes turns at navigating and in spite of their primitive way of life they seem happy, if somewhat bedraggled-looking.

It's past midnight and as a change from the good weather we've been having on other nights when I've stood watch, the rain is coming down in buckets. But I don't mind a bit. Is there anything nicer than being snug and warm indoors and listening to the rain pattering on the roof?

This galley is hotter than blazes. Because of the blackout we have to keep everything tightly sealed. The Germans have become very strict about this now that the Russians are beginning to make it uncomfortable for them. The skipper has told us that we won't be getting our coal supply for a while since all rails and railway cars are to be used for troop transport to the German-Russian border. It's reported that all diplomatic relations with Russia have been broken, which gives the impression that everything is about to blow sky-high.

Very mysterious is a boat loaded with Finnish workers which arrives daily and again leaves for Finland packed with German soldiers. How reassuring it must be for Finland to have such peaceful and amiable neighbors within her borders! Furthermore, there are fairly reliable rumors circulating that the Russians have given an ultimatum to the effect that they will enter the war if an American ship is sunk.

DANZIG

30 May 1941

Dear Mother,

Our supplies are about to run out and they have now put us on German rations. If we didn't have a small reserve stock ourselves, life would be pretty dismal around here. I'm not trying to make things look too bright for us by exaggerating the bad shape the Germans are in, but here are two ships—a Danish and a Swedish—both on German rations. They only work four hours a day because the captain and officers realize that they can't do more on their meager ration. Children are constantly coming on board to beg for food, but this seems to have been going on for quite a while already.

I'm just about being eaten alive by bedbugs and need some more DDT—it seemed to do some good. But if it doesn't finish them off completely this time, an old seaman has told me that the best cure is to sleep in an eiderdown quilt. Couldn't you make me one which would cover me from feet to neck and also make me a hood of mosquito netting so that the whole construction from head to toe would be bedbug-proof?

I'm having a wonderful time and had no idea that I would enjoy life at sea quite as much as I do.

Now I have to start cleaning out the latrines and doing all the little odd jobs which are part of my duties.

Affectionately.

DANZIG
30 May 1941

Dearest Hanne,

The planes are buzzing overhead and are just about driving us crazy. We are watching developments here with bated breath. It sure will be a hot spot to be in when the shooting starts. But there is nothing to worry about as long as you keep your powder dry, as they say.

My shipmates are beginning to get restless, with the result that the population on board is no longer all male. There are always one or two women here, so no one can claim that the crew's quarters are lonely any more. You have no idea what a prostitute in a German port is like. She is no beauty—that's for sure. It's not that I'm shocked. On the contrary, I like to be together with people who are open and honest about things, but I do think that our quarters are getting a bit crowded these days. My mates and I don't quite see eye to eye on the matter of sex and they are anxious to see a picture of the girl who can keep a seaman going on the straight and narrow path even when he's away.

It seems so funny to think that I've known you only a little over a month, seen you about ten times, and never had the chance really to talk to you. Yet I write you my innermost thoughts as if I had known you all my life, because I know that we operate on the same wave length and your heart responds to mine.

I just went outside to see that everything was O.K. The moon has gone to bed and the sun is impatiently waiting to rise.

DANZIG
31 May 1941

I don't know why, but all day I've been in such a wonderful mood—and still am. I've felt on top of the world. You know this happy feeling deep down inside that you have sometimes from the moment your feet hit the floor in the morning until your head hits the pillow at night? In twenty seconds it will be midnight; now in ten and a half. Now I can write June 1, 1941. On New Year's Eve people usually thank each other for the old year which is just over. Since we are both so "young" I shall say instead, "Thank you for the old month and may you have a peaceful and happy new one."

Today I've been on a fierce and bloody hunt for bedbugs. I ripped down all the shelves, took all the bedding and even the boards of my bunk up on deck and put them in the sun. You can imagine what my bunk is like now with only boards and a blanket in it, but if that helps, it's worth the discomfort and I'll keep things this way.

I still feel so wonderful! If I could only convey some of this to you so that we could laugh together across the miles that separate us. It's terrific to be so happy. I seem to get a kick out of the least little thing.

I just went out to see if the lantern is still burning and found everything in order. Hanne, the weather is so marvelous—the sky and the air so crystal clear with millions of stars. The night does such strange things to me.

It's because I'm so happy that I long so terribly for you.

Good night, my love. May you sleep as sweetly as a water lily on a pond.

DANZIG
1 June 1941

Correction: It's already Monday, the second. It isn't so easy to keep track of the days around here. They have a way of sneaking up from behind and taking me by surprise. It's 10 o'clock and I didn't think I'd have the time to write to you tonight, because before my watch began I received orders to move during the course of the night a pile of boards which was lying on one of the hatch covers, and to stack it neatly under the gunwale. I didn't think I'd be through with this job before daybreak, but with you in my heart everything moves with lightning speed.

This, worse luck, is probably my last night on watch. I'm going to miss these pleasant nights with you in this warm little galley. Just think of all the conversations we've had together here.

The birds have given me a hint that day is about to break so I'll stop for tonight. Now all I have to do is to clear up, have a wash and then I'm through. Taking the bedding out of my bunk helped, because last night I only got a single bite. But now my mates are swearing a blue streak because it seems that the bedbugs are making a field day of it in their bunks. It will be fun to see where they end up. Good night, my beloved little girl. You are the light of my life.

DANZIG
2 June 1941

The moon tonight does things to me. There are lots of letters I ought to be writing, but I'm clinging to this single link with you as a bee does to a yellow blossom. This is one of those fantastic nights with a half moon and stars and a transparent sky—not dark blue, but a deep, radiant shade. The trees on the slope stand out against the sky, which is too light to make them appear as black outlines, but rather like fragile, indistinct forms, not quite real. If we could only hold onto the color of the sky at this moment, but it's already begun to fade. Now it's almost gone, but you and I will keep it tucked away in our hearts so that we will be able to take it out and enjoy it exactly the way it was. On the other side the water is full of moonlight, and the rigging of the ship has become a black silhouette stretching upwards. This strange moon has cast such a spell over us.

According to the latest wild rumors today, Russian planes were shot down over Bornholm last night. If it's true, all hell will break loose and it's anybody's guess how long the Germans will last—not long, I hope. What a day it will be when this is all over and we have peace again.

Now, thank God, it's beginning to look as if we might soon get our coal supply, not from Danzig but from Gdynia. We'll be leaving for there shortly. I've had a soft deal as night watchman during the time we've been here, but just the same it isn't exactly this aspect of life at sea which I wanted to get to know.

This afternoon we had a lively discussion on the subject of women. My mates felt that a man can never marry late enough and that he should hold onto his freedom as long as possible. The first officer came out most strongly in defense of this—he is married, by the way. They also claimed that a seaman had no hold over a woman unless she had a flock of kids to keep her busy. I said that there was no more steadying influence on a young fellow than a woman's love and that there is no greater happiness in life than to grow and develop together and have children while you're still young enough to be able to understand them. The boys think I'm a little batty, and that my upbringing has queered my chances of enjoying life.

What would people say if they knew you were getting letters of a hundred pages? The boys here shake their heads and feel sorry for the poor girl who has to suffer through all this. But I couldn't help laughing this afternoon when I went aboard a Danish ship which is anchored right astern of us. Our cook was there and he didn't notice me standing in the door of the galley. The other cook said that he had just written a twelve-page letter to his wife, and our cook said, "On our ship we have a loony guy who writes a hundred." My time is up but I hope that I'll still be on this watch tomorrow night.

. . . Hello. Here I am back again. It's finally been decided that we're shoving off for Gdynia tomorrow to load and from there to Vejle. Marvelous.

Tonight the heat is just about unbearable. There is a scorching wind, but I can't even have the benefit of that since it's impossible to open anything on account of the blackout.

You ought to see the result of my laundry work. I did it all this afternoon but I was in a fix with regard to my shirts because we don't have an iron on board. The first officer, grinning, came to my rescue with a bottle filled with boiling water. Have you ever heard of this before? There's an old saying that a seaman knows the answer to everything. Honestly, when I saw the results I was very much impressed.

This is probably the last evening I'll be able to sit like this and write you for hours on end. Probably I'll never again have the chance to write letters of a hundred pages, so I hope that you'll put up with it just this once.

In a week I'll have a picture of you! I'm going to frame it and nail it up above my bunk, so that you are the last thing I see before falling asleep and the first to smile at me in the morning. You will be a little sun in my life, and you'll be there smiling at me even when things are at their worst.

I just went outside to cool off a bit. The moon is just reaching the edge of the forest, and it reminded me of the last time we were together when it looked the same way.

Something ghastly happened here recently. A German schooner struck a mine not far from port. It went down instantly and only three out of eight were saved. It was too awful for words. Then two days ago a seaman on a Danish ship anchored here got a body caught on his boat hook. The thought is so gruesome that you damn war and all the horrors that go with it, and the thought that the creatures who started this are members of the human race is too terrible to fathom.

Every day that goes by is one day closer to the day when I'll see you again. But I hope that I won't have to bear this agony of waiting much longer.

GDYNIA
6 June 1941

We have reached our destination, so things are beginning to look a bit brighter. We had to lie out at the breakwater because of a bad storm. I've had deck watch as usual, and due to the weather I had to stay on deck from 9 o'clock in the evening until seven the next morning. The first officer and the skipper also took turns on deck so that we would be two men at all times if anything should happen. The night seemed endless and I almost froze to death. The skipper and the first officer were just as frozen but they changed watch every four hours and when they got too cold they could at least go down for a cup of coffee. The first officer and I paced up and down the deck together. He is a clever fellow, courageous and reliable, and it was interesting to hear his ideas on things. We talked about the war, people, religion, women and anything that happened to come up. I learn an awful lot by listening to others even if I don't agree with them. Sometimes I find myself understanding their point of view and I become fond of them, as you always do of people you understand.

When the sun came up things got better. It was a magnificent sunrise with enormous waves in the foreground. When it got to be close to seven I began counting the minutes until I could hit the sack but this unfortunately never came off. Shortly after seven when I had gone down to eat, a tender came out with a pilot on board with instructions to proceed to port. I had to go up on deck again and start working. We had a tough time weighing anchor because of the rough sea. I had every intention of finally getting some sleep right after supper but one of my mates came down with a Pole who spoke Danish. The poor guy was in terrible shape. We, of course, started to talk politics with him.

It seems that in Germany they are tightening their belts to the last notch. They are beginning to be sick of it all and aren't as confident of victory as they used to be. The poor Poles and the prisoners of war are suffering terribly. They are starving, have no clothing, no soap; but worst of all, the Germans treat them with unbelievable brutality, as if they were a herd of cattle. It's too revolting for words, but they take it with a stoic calm, convinced that "he" will be defeated. ("He" is Hitler.) They never say "the Germans" but always "he." I asked the Polish fellow which would be the worse fate, to be under the German or the Russian yoke. He said he couldn't tell because one was the Devil and the other Satan, but that no change could possibly make things worse. "He" had requisitioned this man's house and property and put him in a work camp. The man turned white when he told us about it and shook with rage and emotion. He and his wife had worked hard for twenty years and lived frugally in order to be able to realize their dream. And then, without warning, everything was taken away from them and they were more miserable than ever before. How these poor people can hate! Believe me, we Danes don't know what hatred is, thank God.

RAAGLEJE OR
SOMEWHERE IN THE VICINITY
10 June 1941

At the moment I'm on lookout duty, very comfortably chocked in at the bow and sheltered by the sails. There is a light following wind, and although it's about 8 P.M. the sun is burning my face.

Never have I been on such a wonderful trip as this. We have several mackerel nets out, hoping for a catch, and honestly, despite the load of coal on deck, this is just like a cruise. Everyone is in high spirits at the thought that we will soon be in a Danish port after our month of quarantine in Germany. We have been racing another schooner from Gdynia. The weather has been foul all the way. The moment we stuck our nose outside the harbor I got soaked to the skin. We haven't had much sleep since 11 o'clock Saturday night, because we had to be on deck the whole time in case anything should happen. It's not easy to be at the helm in weather like that, but when you're caught up in the excitement, everything is like a game. Our opponent started from Gdynia two hours ahead of us, and by the time we reached Bornholm we were bow to bow. The other schooner went north of Bornholm while we went south, and unfortunately they gained a lot by that. When we reached Moen the wind died down, so we had to start the engine. It was a race of life and death through the Sound.

Sorry I had to leave you for an hour, but I had to take my turn at the helm. The sun is about to disappear. How I wish you could see this sunset! Hesseloe is right in its path, and as it sinks beneath the blue water—well, this is something that most people are only privileged to see in their dreams and here I have it right in front of me!

I'm going to mail this letter before I reach Vejle—before I have received any of yours. I've put down my thoughts and feelings as they've come and gone, and although I know that many of these things would have been better left unsaid, I feel that we must accept each other the way we are, with the good and the bad—that is, if you feel that way, too. I can only hope for your understanding.

Good-bye for now, my love, and may you continue to be happy.

11 June 1941

We have arrived at Vejle, and I've read your letters. You just can't imagine how relieved I was and how happy you've made me. I think I wrote you yesterday that I wanted to mail this before I had read your letters, but how could I possibly resist the temptation when I was handed three envelopes the moment I got on shore containing everything I've longed for since the last time I saw you. Hanne, Hanne, if only I could be with you at this moment!

If you only knew how I felt after I had read your letters! They showed you to be what you are—sincere and genuine, with no pretense, no glib phrases, just the plain truth. This is to me of infinitely more worth than any declaration of love.

I have bad news. We are leaving Vejle for Finland (Pernavik) and from there to Bandholm and Naestved, so unfortunately you and I won't be seeing each other for some time. "Unfortunately" isn't the word to describe the pain I feel, but if this is our destiny we have to accept it.

FINLAND 3

PERNAVIK, FINLAND
24 June 1941

Dearest Hanne,

We've had a good trip up to now and there are lots of things I ought to tell you, but I can't just now because there are so many more important things happening here. We had two days of thick fog and almost collided with another ship. You narrowly escaped being rid of me for good that time, but strangely enough I wasn't the least bit afraid. It was a big Russian ship which suddenly appeared out of the fog as if a door had opened to let it through. I was on lookout duty and ran off to give the alarm. When I came back to my post, it had disappeared into the fog without a sound. Its mighty hull had towered above us for an instant, and there seemed to be no way of averting a catastrophe. There wasn't a sound; we were proceeding by sail only, and all the usual sounds were as subdued as if they were coming from a great distance.

The next morning in the Finnish bay we met a whole stream of ships all heading for the open sea at full speed. There seemed to be one going by every minute, many only loaded to half their capacity. It was easy to tell by the way they were making their preparations for the sea that they had left the port in great haste. Our skipper was beside himself when he realized that war was about to break out between the Russians and the Finns. After all we had heard at Danzig, there was no doubt about it.

When we arrived here, we were told that if we stayed we did so at our own risk. We stayed and started to load right away, working without sleep or rest until the shooting started. We worked for thirty hours straight and then were completely knocked out for the next twelve. On Monday we started loading at 4 A.M. I worked like a slave at the winch until 9 P.M.

when I crawled down to my bunk more dead than alive and didn't wake up until noon the following day.

Today the Finns are celebrating midsummer, and we are also taking the day off, but only because we're dead beat. You and I had planned that you would fly to Bornholm in four days. I know that this letter won't reach you until long afterwards, but how I hope that you won't go! This is really bad for us and bad for Denmark. We are considered as Germans, and Bornholm is exposed to attack. Who knows when it will be possible to get out of there again? But you must know of all these developments at home.

We have been camouflaged and are anchored close to the cliffs and can only hope that the Russians won't spot us. The British are also bombing Finland. They have their base in Petsamo, so that this is really a dangerous spot to be in. There is another Danish ship here. It passed Hangoe a half-hour before the hostilities began, and couldn't turn back. There are loads of Germans around here and we can't help hoping that they will soon take Hangoe so that we can make an attempt to get out of here. But our deckhand and cook don't want to come along, since there is only a chance of getting through alive. The Russians have a way of machine-gunning the ships —a beastly thing to do since it's always the crew and not the ship that suffers.

If they would have accepted me I would have enlisted as a volunteer, but unfortunately the age requirement is nineteen. I'm all for the Finns in their fight against the Russians. The Finns see how serious their situation is, but they aren't crushed by it. I went ashore the other night; it was impressive to see a whole people united behind a cause. I couldn't help feeling how weak and spineless the Danes are in comparison with them.

Everything is rationed here—only three-quarters of a pint of milk a day! Clothing, shoes, meat—everything is rationed, and the rations are very small. But if a Finn comes on board while we're eating, he proudly says "no thank you" when we offer him something, no matter how hungry he is. Finland wants to hold onto her independence, no matter what, and refuses to accept anything if she feels that she can't reciprocate. If one of them finally does accept, it's always after making absolutely sure that it doesn't cut down our rations and that he won't deprive us of anything.

We're anchored in a sheltered place against the cliffs and the sun is scorching. I'm wearing only shorts and have got quite tanned already. When I get too hot I jump over the side and swim around the ship.

FINLAND
27 June 1941

Dearest Hanne,

I can't, or rather I'm not permitted to write much, and nothing about where we are. We are continually on the move to avoid you know what. Please write even if you don't hear from me. I've written a letter to you which you probably won't get because I wrote a lot of things which I shouldn't have. It's "hot" here and getting "hotter" all the time, but the gods just have to help me get back to you. I can't bear the thought of being separated from you and don't know how I'll get through the time that lies ahead. Please do something for me. Call Mother—you don't need to tell her how bad things look, but only that we may be here for months, perhaps until the war is over.

PERNAVIK
1 July 1941

Darling, I wasn't able to get this letter off to you. All hell has broken loose. The Russians launch their bombing attacks as many as ten times a day, and every time they seem close we have to run for the woods to seek shelter behind the rocks. Things couldn't be much worse, but I haven't felt afraid of dying a single time. Perhaps you are the reason; perhaps it's the knowledge that you're part of me which gives me this feeling of great calm. But how we damn those Russians, because no sooner have we gotten into our bunks than we have to get out again and tear into the woods. One night we had to run for shelter four times, and we cursed them with the vilest oaths we could think of.

I'm on night watch again and am sitting on the deck cargo as I'm writing this. The nights up here are almost as bright as day and already the sun is about to appear.

About ten minutes ago three big Russian planes flew over us. They dropped a lot of bombs on the sawmill just on the other side of the cape where we were anchored. Every time the sirens go off, I have to call the others and everyone gathers on deck. There we stand and gaze up at the monsters which majestically glide across the sky. If they change their course, we jump into the launch and haul ourselves ashore and head for the woods, where we are slowly eaten alive by mosquitoes. Oh, how we hate these bastards! One of the cabin boys, the deckhand and the cook are scared to death and so out of their minds that it's impossible to talk to them. I wonder what will happen to us if we have to stay here until the war is over.

I wish you could have been here last night! The Finns shot down two Russian planes over the woods. We were all on deck cheering. Two giants like this, silently moving among the clouds and dropping their bombs without being in the least affected by the anti-aircraft artillery, are a terrifying thing to see. When I see the death and destruction they spread over innocent people, a feeling of futile, choking fury besets me and I'd give anything to get right in there and fight them. Thank

God that this isn't happening in Denmark, and that you aren't exposed to the awful, nervous strain of not feeling safe a single hour out of twenty-four.

As I sit here I can hear the distant roar of cannons. But through all the hell—the bedbugs which are eating me alive, mosquitoes, bombs, sleepless nights because of the alarms—through it all you're never out of my consciousness for a second.

I'm running out of lots of things including shoes and have just finished making myself a pair out of old ropes which will serve the purpose for the time being.

Yesterday afternoon I took a long walk through the woods to the tip of the peninsula. I stood for a long time watching the movements of the Russian planes, which had just finished bombing Lovisa. When they were out of sight I undressed and put my clothes on the upper branches of a small pine tree which I carefully navigated into the water. Then I jumped in and transported my stuff to a little island about a mile away. Here I stretched out and dozed on the warm rocks in the sun. I enjoyed it all the more after my swim. From there I swam to the next peninsula, got into my clothes, and went back to the ship. How wonderful it was to be able to be myself for once.

We've just had another air raid. What a blessing it would be to be out of this whole mess or else really take part in it. Sitting on the sidelines like this is unbearable. Oh, Hanne, how I wish you were here with me! I would forget the horror all around me and just be happy, and my only aim would be to make you just as happy. I would give up all this useless fretting and trying to make any sense out of all that is happening, and I would no longer be aware of all the stress and strain we are under.

There go the sirens again!

PERNAVIK
6 July 1941

Bombs, Russians, machine guns and anti-aircraft have become the things we live by. I went ashore with one of the boys for a while last night. When we were in the middle of a field, the Russians started to bomb the sawmill which was only about twelve hundred feet from where we were taking shelter. It rained stones, trees and splinters all around us and we were a sorry sight covered from head to toe with mud and mire. I've never been so crazy mad. It was more than I could bear to lie there and watch this insane destruction without being able even to raise my little finger to prevent it.

Last night I was on watch again and we had to go ashore twice because of the Russians. Then this morning when I had got into my bunk and had just about fallen into a deep sleep, I had to leap out of bed and back on shore again. Two hours later I was back in my bunk and this time I had two hours' sleep. Then up and out again. It seems an eternity since I've been able to sleep for three hours straight. After a while you become obsessed with the idea of just being able to lie down and sleep in the absolute assurance of not being disturbed for the next eight hours. No one around here does much work during the day; most of our time is spent dozing on deck in the sun.

Can you possibly imagine what such an attack is like? Three enormous Russian planes came flying over us at an altitude of a couple of miles. They always climb just as high even when they're dropping bombs. I used to think that they would come with an insane speed and then disappear in a few seconds. Have you tried to follow the movements of a plane which seems suspended like a tiny dot up there? You can clearly see its outline despite the altitude, but it moves so slowly that you're hardly aware of any motion whatsoever and—

Excuse the interruption. We had to go back on land again, but nothing happened. They disappeared behind a cloud. Now I forgot what I wanted to tell you. Well, this plane slowly and majestically glides across the sky like a big glittering bird of prey. A piercing whistle cuts the air and a second later there is an explosion and you see earth, rocks and perhaps even a house fly up in the air a few hundred yards from you. And after the explosion the long drawn-out whistle of the bomb, which has already fallen, continues. You stare fixedly at the monsters overhead. They slowly glide away as if nothing at all had happened. You look at your watch and see to your amazement that the whole thing has taken only two minutes, but if you ask yourself how long this lasted, you would be willing to swear that it was several hours.

We are fishing like mad and put out fifty lines every night because our food supply is just about down to rock-bottom. The Finnish rations are pitiful. They get less than a pound of meat a month, which is next to nothing.

Good morning—it's now Monday, July 7, 1941, 4:10 A.M. I just woke my mates up and they have gone off to fish. It's a wonderful morning. The sun is just coming up and is warming the air nicely. To begin where I left off yesterday, I spent a good night—full moon and only one alert. After the all clear had sounded last night, four of us went ashore. Naturally we met some terrific girls. None of them was over seventeen. I can't for the life of me figure out why, but they seemed to take to us and before we knew it even the most timid of them had us playing some sort of boy-catches-girl game. You'll laugh.

but we all had a wonderful time. The girls were cute and lots of fun once they had got over their shyness, and they all were so graceful and well put together. They seem to have taken a special shine to me, because they keep on inviting me to rowing and bicycle parties and lots of other things. My mates are jealous as hell. But I'm not going to try to make myself out to be better than I am. I'm as proud as a peacock over it, no matter how hard I try to put myself in my place. I don't quite understand the reason why, but after something like this all my thoughts go straight to you, Hanne, and I feel so incredibly happy.

PERNAVIK
7 August 1941

Yesterday I got a package. It was brought to me by the Danish ambulance and contained letters, chocolate, soap—everything I needed most. Mother wrote me that they needed men in the ambulance corps and wondered whether I couldn't get permission from the skipper to join until our ship can leave. I wanted to do this very much but I couldn't get the authorization. The skipper said that if we were sent home I could ask whether they could still use me. Hanne, please don't think that this desire on my part to join the ambulance corps means that I don't long for you as much as ever, and I hope you'll understand this and not feel hurt or neglected. But when I see what sacrifices the Finns are making here, I know we must do our part by postponing our reunion until the right moment comes.

PERNAVIK
9 August 1941

Dear Mother,

My finger hurts like hell. The nail came off, although the finger hadn't been bothering me for a long time, and now it's raw and keeps on bleeding all the time. I think it's the beginning of an abscess, and this is probably due to lack of nourishment.

Thanks for your letters. It was wonderful to have news from home. I'm in good spirits and in many ways I'm enjoying life here. Most of the boys are getting a little nervous, although "going off their rocker" would describe their mental state far better. The only thing I want is to get back to Hanne. Never would I have believed that feelings could be so strong, and the intensity of these feelings have made me into a new and more mature person. My mind is filled with new thoughts and my life has a deeper meaning. I know these are big-sounding words for my age, but you know what I mean, Mother; you understand what I feel.

What you said about Hanne made me very happy—happier than you will ever know—and I want to thank you. You talk about my coming home and going back to school, and I must admit that I would like to, though for very different reasons than you think. But still, I feel that I must continue this way of life which I've begun, because the sea makes me feel at home. Sometimes it seems as if it would be impossible for me to continue to be separated from my little girl. But deep down I know that this is the only life for me, and I also know that much happiness will come our way and make up for the things we'll miss. It must seem to you that we are far too young to know what we want. But I am very, very sure, and I think that Hanne's mind is also made up, and I doubt if either of us will ever change our minds.

The time spent here has done a lot for me. The constant danger and the uncertainty have given me a lot to think about and taught me a great deal. I'm the only one who continues to sleep on deck despite the cold and the rainstorms. I've made myself a little tent out of an old piece of canvas, which helps to some extent, but I've discovered that wet blankets can be warm once I'm snugly rolled up in them. If the sea is calm, the mosquitoes devour you wherever you are, but think of the feeling of freedom when looking up and seeing the stars!

M.S. *Johanne* PERNAA PR. LOVISA, FINLAND
10 August 1941

Dearest Nitte,

I've just been reading *Wind, Sand and Stars* and it made me feel the way you do when you walk in the fields after the rain has washed the air. I was reading about the little pond near Punta Arenas, which had the strange characteristic of rising and receding with the tide and following the rhythm of the ocean. Suddenly the scene changed and my thoughts strayed from the book and I found myself in a little house on Kragevej. And who is sitting on the sofa with her legs tucked under her? You! We were discussing this book and you found such vivid expressions to describe it and put my feelings about it into words. Remember? And you remember how we talked about man and his destiny? I remember it all so well. Fond memories like this compensate me for not being with you all, and they often affect me more deeply than did the incident itself. This is where I wandered off, and while I was sitting here remembering all this, a gift came down out of the blue which made me very happy—a greeting from you. Thank you, Nitte. It touched me deeply that it should arrive at the moment when you were in my thoughts, and I was still more moved after having read your letter. Thank you. You couldn't have made me happier.

Autumn is here with its storms and rough weather and we're crawling into our holes like bears ready to hibernate. It's lonely here although there are several of us, but my thoughts are free to wander off to gayer places, Loendal, Denmark, and all of you back home. I'm deeply grateful for the love and devotion you've all lavished on me since the day I was born. Until now I never realized what it meant.

What made me happiest of all was what you wrote about the girl for me. These were the words I had been hoping to hear. I knew that they would come, but they were more heartfelt than anything I had dared to hope for.

Write me soon. I hope that too much time won't go by before we meet again.

PERNAVIK
10 August 1941

Dearest Hanne,

Autumn is here with its thunderstorms and bad weather. The clouds pile up in blue-black masses and burst over our heads, drenching everything with great thoroughness. I'm still sleeping on deck since it would be hopeless down below in the bedbug nursery which is now my bunk.

Lately the first officer and I have been doing some fishing in our spare time. There is something exciting about having to go out in all kinds of weather to attend to our lines.

A couple of days ago two girls of about fifteen or sixteen came aboard to pay us a visit. The first officer gave them permission to look around the ship—he and I were alone on board. They stayed and listened to records until about 4 o'clock, but when it got to be time for them to leave, the little chicks suddenly began to think about how dark it was getting and that the woods were full of Russians. (The Russians are parachuting more and more men, but they are being picked off at about the same rate they come down.) Of course the first officer and I offered to take them home.

You should have seen the little blonde number who attached herself to me. She had swiped a little model ship which the night watchman had carved during the night. On the way she asked if I had made it, and I said yes, for the hell of it. She asked me if she could keep it as a souvenir to remember me by. I said yes but couldn't help grinning, so she was very peeved at me. I don't know why, since I gave her the darned thing. The first officer always calls me "lange" (the tall one) when we're alone, and she immediately took that to be my last name—Kim Lange. I had such a hard time keeping a straight face.

After we had deposited them on their doorsteps, we swore that if ever a girl set foot on board again we would send her home to her mother while it was still light. They lived eight miles away, so our renown had apparently spread far and wide. These girls came an awfully long way just to swim off our cliffs. The people around here claim that this has never happened before, but now all nonsense is over for this year.

One thing did click. One of my mates fell for the postmaster's daughter, and although I'm sure that it's just a light case on his part, I wish them all the best just the same.

Yesterday a Finnish patrol shot an old man, thinking that he was a Russian. They fired without warning, and the first officer and I narrowly escaped the same fate. Like the old man we were out berry-picking. It was the white cap of the first officer which saved us, and how we bless that cap! The Finnish sergeant who was the leader of that patrol exclaimed, "How lucky we are that he wasn't a Dane." The fellow had just got a stripe because his patrol had picked off so many Russians, and it seemed that the idea that he could have been demoted bothered him more than the thought that he might have shot one of us. They are hard as nails, these Finns. Thank God I don't have to fight against them.

PERNAVIK
12 August 1941

Today we picked blueberries and also played a game of knives, and this morning Paul and I took a half-hour off and went for a swim. The weather was wonderful and the water not too cold. Tonight the first officer and I went to put our lines out. When we had rowed for about a half-hour, we got into a thick fog. After we were through we started to row against the wind hoping that it wouldn't shift. When we reached shore, we had to ask where we were and in what direction we should follow the coastline in order to get back. It was awfully cold, but when you're rowing you can stand it. When I got back on board, I made a dozen traps which I'm going to set tomorrow.

PERNAVIK
15 August 1941

Just as I sat down to take in this fabulous sunrise and felt as far away from the human race and its lunacies as if I had been on another planet, there went that whistling sound from a falling bomb again.

Yesterday morning we all worked like slaves, spreading our sails so that they would dry and then taking them down and stowing them away. It was a lot of fun but hard work. I don't think we've lost our physical fitness during this period of idleness. On the contrary, the swimming has put us in good shape, although we can't help noticing how much we miss the hard daily routine.

In the afternoon we set my traps. Unfortunately there was nothing in them when I went up to look last night, although some of them were closed and there were some stains around.

I think that the steel wire I used was too heavy. Well, old pal, I see that I have to stop for today.

PERNAVIK
20 August 1941

Today it's two months since we came here—the two best months of the year. Still they've dragged and we have four to go—don't ask me how. Today for the first time I saw a ship. It came right after lunch with all sails rigged and the engine at full speed. It seemed to be coasting around the islands here. After they had dropped anchor right next to us, a man came on board and told us that he was out of fuel and would have to call for a tugboat. Suddenly his face lit up as if the bright idea had just occurred to him that perhaps he would be able to buy some from us. We said no, whereupon he rowed back to his ship, started up the engine and steamed off. Amazing how fast he got over his lack of fuel. So much better for him, but they certainly are bold, these Finns.

I'm still not catching anything in my traps, but it doesn't matter. I get all the thrills of the sport, enjoy nature and have a lot of fun studying the habits of animals.

This afternoon three Russian planes flew overhead. The clouds were low and they flew under them the way the Germans did on April 9th.[1] This time we all got really scared. We could even distinguish their machine guns, etc., and they came overhead so fast that by the time we saw them it was too late to go ashore. We scrambled for shelter where we could find it, and you should have seen us afterwards, crawling out of our holes, one by one, like prairie dogs, making sure that the danger was over.

The boys have been to Lovisa where lots of things were hap-

[1] The date of the German invasion of Denmark and Norway.

pening and they came back full of news. While they were at a café there was a raid. When they returned to the ship, the rest of us greeted them so eagerly you would think they were coming back from an expedition to another country. They told us how terrible everything was: not a window left in town. They had all been replaced by boards and cardboard. It was all so dreary and depressing as people have had to cut down to the barest necessities. It's awful to see such an independent people forced to lead the life of cave dwellers.

At the barber's the boys have been reading *Signal* which contained a long series of propaganda articles with pictures of Danes from Copenhagen who went to Germany "to participate in the creation of a new Europe." We all agreed that it's high time we have a revolution at home—in the best Mexican style. Now I'm heading for my bunk, practically asleep already. Good night!

M.S. *Johanne*
PERNAA PR. LOVISA
27 August 1941

Dearest Mother,

You write that I have so much to be happy and grateful for that I can't let myself get so down in the dumps. You're right, Mother, but try to put yourself in my place. I knew Hanne for seven days—*seven days*! I felt as if she had always been part of my life—and then to be separated from her for seven months! It's terribly hard on me, especially since I have no work to occupy me at the moment, but I'm not really unhappy and I'm not complaining, only terribly impatient. Sometimes I almost go out of my mind and feel that I've got to find an outlet for all that is dammed up inside me.

You ask how I lost my nail—God only knows. Suddenly it came off. It was the one I jammed the first day I was on board, but now it's just about O.K. Abscesses: I've got three of them—two at the waist and one on the leg. The two on my back weren't so bad, but the one on my leg was big and hurt all the way up to the groin. Strangely enough nothing came out even when I cut it, but it gradually disappeared by itself. At the time I didn't feel so good but now I'm fine again.

What you wrote about Hanne and me pleased me very much. I would have understood your feelings if you hadn't been prepared to take it too seriously at first. But Mother, you must learn to love my future wife as you love Ruth. I wish that she could come and go as freely as Ruth and I do at home. I know this is asking a lot, but you do understand, don't you? I don't mind your discussing her, but it must be openly and naturally and not in a gossippy way. I would like so much for the family to know her, so that she won't be a stranger to you when I come home. She is the most natural girl you could possibly imagine and must be treated in an easy and casual way.

What did Ruth think about her? This really must have been a subject for discussion between you, and I bet that Ruth reminded you of what you have been saying all along—that we should wait until we're older. Do you remember my saying even before I met Hanne that I felt I would like to get married at an early age? How strange that the whim of fate so quickly took me at my word. Mother, isn't the fact that I'm as happy as any human being can be, proof enough for you?

PERNAVIK

28 August 1941

I slept below deck last night and the bedbugs just about drove me crazy. I felt them crawling all over me, but if I was able to get used to them once, I suppose I can again.

It's been raining most of the day and we've whiled away

the time by playing chess. We've become avid players lately. It's a good way to make the time go quickly, and besides, it's good mental exercise. The first officer came down and asked sarcastically if we didn't think we were being overworked. "Yes, here," said one of the fellows and slapped his rear end. Roaring laughter! It doesn't take much to set us off these days.

29 August 1941

They have now given us life belts, and we're supposed to keep them on at all times until the worst is over. The skipper went ashore and was told by the shipowners that we should be prepared to take off in two weeks. I feel as if I'd just gotten my release from prison. We have provisions and warm clothing on the raft as well as in the launch, and we have an enormous amount of work to do within the next few days. But the work will seem like a game because every minute of it brings me closer to my girl. I only hope that all goes well and that the Russians won't spot us.

Soon I shall be on your doorstep, my darling. Until then.

PERNAVIK

30 August 1941

One night we were standing around waiting for the bus. The first one I saw came around the last curve at top speed and came to a sudden stop. The people were standing ready to jump off, because everything has to move with lightning speed. The windows of the bus had blackout curtains so hardly any light escaped. Before the bus had stopped, the door opened and a pretty girl in uniform jumped out. I caught a glimpse of the inside of the bus and saw a sea of faces—hard boiled soldiers, a woman with a child in her arms, all with that faraway look so typical of passengers in moving vehicles. I especially remember a boy—he couldn't have been more than seventeen—with heavy boots, uniform, and the inevitable loaded rifle between his knees. This wasn't what made me unable to forget him. It was his terrible rasping cough. I only saw him those few moments when the bus stopped, but his cough, the expression on his face, affected me so strangely. It seemed as if a glimpse of a whole human life opened up before me during the flash of a second. Then the lights went out and the bus started moving. The last thing I saw was the young girl standing on the running board and looking back at us. Then she, too, disappeared as the bus went around the bend with a last roar from the exhaust. At that moment I seemed to wake up and be transported back to the moment before the bus came. Everything was the same, there was the tinkling of a cowbell in the distance, and from a house nearby came the sound of a child wailing. All was quiet and peaceful. At that moment a small group of people were moving along the highway and there was nothing I could share with them except a rasping cough. It made me feel so funny inside.

PERNAVIK

1 August 1941

Tonight the rain has been coming down in buckets. I took the blacksmith and Paul over to Pernaa and then turned around and sailed back. I rolled my pants up over my knees and took off my oilskin and my sou'wester. I sat there with my chin resting on my knees, not moving. There was hardly a breeze. The sea was calm as it always is when it rains like this. I listened to the sea and the rain. How restful it is, and how still and peaceful! I was dreaming and my thoughts didn't have to reach out for you because you were right here in the boat with me. Have you ever watched a drop of water, or rather a drop of rain, as it hits the water? I was sitting there holding your wet hand in mine and feeling so happy and light-hearted. The thing I wanted most was to sail out on the open sea with you, so that you would get to know the fresh, salty smell of the ocean and feel the froth of a big breaker.

Was in Borgaa yesterday. The place was full of drunken soldiers from the Hangoe front. They were all talking about how terrible it was there, and saying that few ever got away from there alive and that you had to be careful not to advance too quickly during the attack, etc. On the market place tipsy soldiers tried to stow a buddy in even worse condition into a bus bound for Helsingfors. But the people inside shoved him right out again. His buddies swore and shouted that when they were on their way to the front, people were more than willing to make room for them, but behind the front—well, that was a different story.

It was easy to see how the war had already marked them. Every day brings with it more evidence of the fact that Man has gone completely berserk. He has enough intelligence to know that what he is doing is mad, but still he goes right ahead. How insane it all is!

The bus was stopped by a patrol both coming and going. Jens and I didn't have passes, but pulled out our Danish passports. Time and again we were asked if we were volunteers and saw the disappointment in their faces when we had to admit that we weren't.

I'm trying hard to stop swearing. I've gotten pretty much into the habit, and it's not going to be easy to break when every second word around here is a cuss word. It's not on any moral grounds, but I suddenly realized that it's a sign of weakness and lack of education to let myself be influenced by my surroundings to that extent.

PERNAVIK
1 September 1941

Happy days are back and everyone is in high spirits because we're going to sea again and also because we have something to do at last.

Just think! In a month we'll be back in the world again. Now I'm packing boards around the bridge to protect it from machine gun bullets and also getting the launch and the raft ready.

They have just issued us our life belts which we're not supposed to leave out of sight during the trip, but I have a feeling that everything will be O.K.

24 September 1941

We weighed anchor around 10 o'clock and made for the dock where our coal load was waiting. We got an electric cable on board so now we have light again. On Monday the oiler and I went to Lovisa on Johan's bicycle. Don't ask me how, but I managed to puncture a tire four times on the way home. We rode through a landscape so beautiful that it's hopeless even to try to describe it. Why couldn't you have been along? There were steep climbs and sharp curves around the cliff, and beyond every curve something new and exciting. The oiler got a little revolver which I hope to buy from him later on. We tried it out yesterday and it's a gem.

28 September 1941

This afternoon I washed clothes for all I was worth. There was an invasion of kids from around here watching me—some from the pier, and some of them even came on board. To celebrate the King's birthday we dressed ship. The effect was striking with the mountains, the woods and the sea as a background, and a clear blue sky as a frame around it all.

PERNAA PR. LOVISA
16 October 1941

Dear Mother,

Already we have snow, skis have made their appearance all over and it's bitterly cold.

You asked me to tell you something about my shipmates, but that's a tough assignment.

1. Seaman Jens Rasmussen is intelligent, steady and reliable; impossible to throw him out of balance. In many ways he and I have the same tastes and the same way of going about things.

2. Oiler Johannes Nelsen is small, fat, has a wonderful disposition and is full of fun. He always seems to be picking a fight but is basically a good guy. He has no education to speak of, but nevertheless he has a very decided opinion on everything.

3. Apprentice Seaman Olaf Pedersen, a boy of eighteen, but you would take him for fifteen—he seems to be afraid of his own shadow. His mother, who brought him up together with three sisters, apparently treated him as one of them, and—to make it worse—he was the youngest. But perhaps he'll become a man some day when the influence of all these women has worn off.

4. Mechanic Paul Theillade, honest and reliable; never sees anything bad in anyone. He is so convinced of the innate goodness of people that you can't help having the highest respect for him. He is the best friend anyone could wish for and he has a wonderful sense of humor. Most characteristic of him is his willingness to help another fellow out. He and I have watch together and have a fine time.

PERNAVIK
30 October 1941

Dearest Hanne,

We had all turned in and the lights were out. I had just had a skirmish with Paul, and when peace was about restored, someone came on board with a flashlight—it was the blacksmith. He came in to tell us about a telegram which had just arrived saying, "Follow *Vaering.*" It was a long time before we could calm down after that message. They woke us up at 6 A.M. the next morning and we worked all day to get two cords of wood, water, provisions, etc., on board.

HELSINGFORS
1 November 1941

We sailed around 8 o'clock. We saw an isolated mine, but the weather was so clear that there was no great danger of running into any. We are now anchored outside *Vaering* and astern of *Clytia.*

When we arrived in Helsingfors we had coffee and then went to a Finnish steam bath for a good scrubbing. First we came into a room where we were washed by some old women. From there we went into the showers and finally into the steam bath, where they gave us a birch twig to beat ourselves with. There was a huge oven with some big stones on top over which we had to pour water to make the steam. We were completely bushed when we got out of there.

M.S. *Johanne*
NIELSON & THORDEN, SHIPOWNERS
FABIANSGATAN 6, HELSINGFORS
10 November 1941

Dear Grandfather,

Thanks for your letter. I had been looking forward to hearing from you and Paula for a long time and I appreciated it very much.

You ask what I've been doing since I've been here. First of all, lots of things have happened which haven't appeared in the papers, but unfortunately I can't go into them here. When we came here we were the only ship in the bay. The same morning the others left in a frightful hurry, some with only half their cargo on board, and in whatever state of readiness they happened to be. The shipowners hadn't given our skipper any orders, so we began to load, hoping to finish in spite of everything. We loaded for forty-eight hours without stopping, which is possible up here during the summer months. I operated the winch and during this time I was only off my post for four hours' sleep. It was a lot of fun—especially in retrospect.

Warmest greetings.

M.S. *Johanne*
NIELSON & THORDEN, SHIPOWNERS
FABIANSGATAN 8, HELSINGFORS
10 November 1941

Dear Nitte,

I just got your letter and at the same time found out that I could pick up the book at the shipowners tomorrow. Many thanks. You don't know how happy I was to hear from you again.

The stupidity of the human race is appalling. I've heard both men and women say in a hopeless, despairing way, "Where do you find happiness in this world? Is it possible to be happy even if you don't find the one great love?" But where is happiness if not within oneself? The logic of this occurred to me for the first time one morning when I saw the sun rise. First I felt that I was unable to absorb this wonderful spectacle and this made me ask myself why. I came to the conclusion that it is indifference and inertia on my part which makes me bypass beautiful things—they may be in the form of a thought, an animal or a human being—countless times without seeing the wonder that is there for me. How could I possibly hope to experience this particular sunrise when I continually pass by so many things which exist for me, without giving them even a fleeting thought? Wasn't it intended that we live as fully as possible and with our eyes wide open? That morning I knew that for an instant I had been given an insight into something very rare and precious, and perhaps because of it I have become a little wiser.

I've become aware of the same thing in my relationship with Hanne, and I know that I have her to thank for that sunrise.

The thoughts that mill around in my head don't stem from a desire to take myself seriously but from an instinct as deep as life itself. It's a searching without a purpose, an unexplainable hunger, and I think it must be the unconscious striving for truth.

HELSINGFORS
10 November 1941

Dearest Hanne,

This morning about 2 o'clock a woman came creeping down here. She wanted to make a little "deal." We told her that she could sleep in the galley if she didn't have any place else to go, but then she ambled off again. There are thousands who live a life like this—why? Then slowly it hit me with full force how abundant and extravagant nature really is. How many wild flowers wither and die every year. It's the way of life, and I know that I haven't fully appreciated all the wonderful gifts life lavishes on us. Suddenly I felt a fondness well up inside me for this woman. How much she was willing to give of herself and how much the poorest creature is capable of giving! Isn't there something great about a person who accepts her own worth and what she can give, as such a matter of course that she isn't even conscious of it? And so it is with this woman —she isn't aware of her own worth.

I can almost see you now. You're smiling, perhaps even laughing out loud, and you're saying to yourself, "And he wrote something about not taking himself too seriously." I do hope you're not laughing at me because it would mean that you don't understand what I mean. When we are joking we're apt to say that we're really serious-minded by nature, but am I being too solemn and serious because I feel something very strongly or because something forces itself up from the bottom of my heart? This evening my love for you is so strong that I almost don't dare to think about it. It's like when we think of the time when we'll be together—but there I go being serious again!

M.S. *Johanne*
FABIANSGATAN 6, HELSINGFORS
25 November 1941

Dear Nitte,

Today I got two letters and both were from you. Funny that both you and Hanne should feel at the same time that I'm in a state of upheaval. But even if this comes from the two of you, it isn't quite so. What concerns me at the moment is due to entirely different reasons and both have to do with Hanne. This began when I fell in love with her. Suddenly I was able to open up and bring some of my innermost feelings out into the light of day and this made them clearer to me.

At Stenhus they always told me that I idled away my time daydreaming. But what is daydreaming really? Sometimes I've lain awake half the night trying to think something through which was bothering me, and in the classroom a thought might come to my mind which would take me far away. They would scold me, but I isolated myself behind a wall and what they said didn't matter. They said that I was snooty, lazy, a dreamer and many other things, but I didn't pay any attention to them. Something more important was trying to work itself out, ideas and thoughts of far more value to me than all the book learning in the world. But I do admit that these things would probably never have come to me at this age, had I not learned and been guided by books.

Can you see how very happy I am now to know at the age of eighteen that what I was groping for then has turned out to be the right way for me? So my time wasn't completely wasted after all. I realize that to you, Hanne and Mother it may seem as if I have changed. Perhaps it may be true with regard to how I express myself and the way I act, but my approach to things hasn't changed. I'm the same person today as I was as far back as I can remember—even going back to my childhood in Canada. I've just come to realize one very important thing since then—perhaps it was just as well not to be aware of this earlier—and that is the tremendous value of books. I used to prefer finding things out for myself rather than from others. I'm not trying to say that the books I've read have accomplished miracles, but on board they have certainly influenced the thinking of my shipmates in many ways and made them into better men. They feel this themselves, and look forward almost as much as I do to my book packages.

My time is about up. Keep well, and thanks for everything.

Affectionately.

HELSINGFORS

28 November 1941

Dearest Hanne,

Recently I've been doing some thinking about religion, but I haven't written anything about it to you because I didn't quite know how.

There was the time when people believed in the gods Odin and Thor, and they believed in them with just as much conviction as any minister of the gospel believes in Christianity. Then man made some progress, became more civilized, and in accordance with natural law his religion and faith kept pace with this development. One day we will be looking at Christianity in its present state the way we now look at the gods of our ancestors. I can't help feeling sometimes that all religion is an expression of a certain cowardice in man. Perhaps you've noticed that the only things we humans fear are the things we don't know and understand. Therefore we must find a way to explain them, and this explanation upon which we build everything we call religion. Tradition means everything to man. Take education, for instance. You would be strong if behind you there was a family tradition going back a thousand years; how much stronger you would be than your brother and sister if they had broken with this tradition. I'm quite certain that you would stand secure where they would be uncertain.

I realize that the weak must have laws to guide them; otherwise there would be no difference between them and animals. They must have laws spelled out because they need promises of reward or punishment, without which they are lost. On the other hand, the man who is strong can make his own laws. He has within himself the ability to obey them without the need of punishment or reward. He knows that nature fulfills these laws without any unnatural, let alone supernatural, explanation. The man who is strong knows that in adhering to his laws and his instincts the greatest reward he can have is the satisfaction and joy which his constant spiritual growth will give him. I don't mean that I don't believe in eternal life, but I believe in a different way from most people. To me, Paradise is a magic word which helps to make death easier for the old and the weak. To me, this seems too much like wishful thinking. I believe in eternal life through our children, but perhaps even more through our actions in this life.

I'm convinced that a man of noble spirit can die perfectly happy and at peace if he can look back on a life of good deeds and if he has learned to govern himself. I don't think that we're too far from realizing the responsibility which is ours in life: that we are a link in the chain of evolution and that we, each time we break a moral law, weaken and tear down what our children and grandchildren are going to build on. There is so much about life which we will never understand, but I'm also convinced that most things are much simpler than we think. The laws of nature are beautiful in their simplicity, while man's laws are involved and complicated.

HELSINGFORS
6 December 1941

We went to the swimming pool, which is very slick, and it was wonderful to do some swimming again. The surprising thing about the Finnish steam baths and swimming pools is the free and easy way in which the women move about among the men in the baths and dressing rooms.

Today is Finland's independence day, so we have a holiday like everyone else. It's snowing and everything is freezing up, which makes me pretty sure that we won't get the ship out of here. There are four mine sweepers docked right beside us and for the past few days they've been having gunnery practice. I never fully realized to what extent the Germans are slaves. To judge from the noise coming from their ships you would think that it was recreation hour in a schoolyard. You may think that this is an exaggeration, but imagine if you can each man shouting at the top of his lungs. I've never heard anything like it. At one point I saw five or six men wildly running around the deck followed by an enraged dog. You can't help being sorry for them, because they are stupid enough to give their lives for something which is going to destroy them, their children and all of us. The darkness they live in is so complete that they actually believe in their own screaming that they are fighting for justice. They lack any personal will and courage when it comes to defending their own ideas and aims, and let themselves be transformed into ersatz people. It's appalling to think that stupidity can rule an entire people who have so many good qualities, to the extent that they are unable to have a single independent and personal thought. It's horrible to hear them. No matter where they are they scream and howl as if all hell had broken loose.

HELSINGFORS
13 December 1941

Dearest Paula and Grandfather,

Once more Christmas is here, and we had been hoping so very much to be home for the holidays. But to begin at the beginning. A week ago we received orders to get under way immediately. We started preparations to leave the same evening and at 4:30 the next morning we were already working away in pitch darkness, snow and freezing cold to furl our heavy winter sails. At 7 o'clock we were finished with all the sails with the exception of the spanker. Everyone was in high spirits and we were all excited at the prospect of getting the ship home for Christmas.

Shortly before 8 A.M. a hawser was handed on board and the icebreaker pulled us around until we were in the clear. Then came the turn of the other schooner and the steamer, which left first. We followed at a distance of a couple of hundred yards, and last in this tiny Danish convoy came the schooner.

In the beginning we made very little headway—sometimes none at all. There was something exciting about gliding through such an icy wasteland. When we had been moving for about an hour and a half the steamer signaled with the siren that it was going to move in reverse. We stopped our engine and waited. The siren sounded three times and each time the steamer tried to go in reverse. But it was no good. They were stuck. In the meantime we kept moving back and forth to avoid getting stuck ourselves. The steamer soon gave up trying to break loose on its own and our skipper realized that we would never get through with the little fuel we had. After they had communicated with each other by loudspeaker, we moved forward to the small opening left by the wake of the ship and after much maneuvering we were able to turn around and pass the schooner with a distance of less than twenty feet, so that both ships could stay in the clear. Hardly three hours after we had left the port we were back again. We had a hard time approaching the pier because of the blocks of ice but we finally made it. The steamer doesn't seem to have gotten through yet.

The same day we made applications for visas to return home by land and we had pinned all our hopes on getting home for Christmas, but unfortunately the red tape takes longer than we had thought. All sails had to be lowered again—if possible, clear of snow as they were furled, but this was next to impossible since it was snowing hard. Then we had to get the ship ready for the winter which was a big job and especially hard because of the freezing weather, but we are just about through and these last days before we leave we're going to saw enough wood so that the first officer, who has to stay on board, will have enough. Just now the others came and gave me the sad news that the steamer which had tried to force its way through the ice will never get back to port.

My fondest greetings to you.

Affectionately.

DANISH INTERLUDE 4

KRAGEVEJ, HELLERUP
6 January 1942

My dear Nitte,

Will you forgive me for not having written sooner? I wanted so much to tell you how very happy I am. You can probably imagine what it meant to me to get home. When I arrived at the main station I phoned Hanne. She told me that Mother had just invited her to breakfast. We decided to meet at the station and not let anyone know that I had arrived. Our meeting at the station was somewhat different from what I had imagined it would be. It was much less emotional than I had pictured it, but at the same time much more moving.

You can't imagine the excitement at home when I walked in behind Hanne. When I had been in the house for three minutes, it seemed impossible that I had been in Sweden the same day and seen Stockholm with all its Christmas lights and that I had been a novice on board the *Johanne* only two days before. I could hardly believe it. The whole Finnish trip already seems so terribly far away.

You say that you have your doubts that I'll find much time to read during the next few years. That I can't say, but I do know that it's always possible to find the time if you really want to, even if you're dead beat or in a bad mood.

Nitte, in one of your letters you wrote, "Always keep moving forward, never get bogged down. Make a mental note of what particularly interests you most in order to be able to return to it later on." I wonder if you realize just how true your words are? I've thought about them a lot lately. Slowly I've made some progress on the road to eternal life; it's only a step but it's forward. We become all wrapped up in our prejudices, in ourselves, and in the thousands of little things which constitute our daily life. Time and again these past few years I've been aware that by the magnificent generosity of nature, every little thing has been planned to serve our greatest good—like the seed which is the beginning of each living thing. Just as simple and just as beautiful is each little event of our life, put there by design to create the conditions which will bring more satisfaction and more real happiness. This thought makes me appreciate life itself even more than ever before. It makes me accept each little occurrence at its real value and makes my life full of excitement and interest.

Here I am writing page after page, but I can't ever seem to express a fraction of all the things I would like to share with you. But you see, though, that when I get a few lines from you, I have enough food for thought to last a long time. More than once you have given me advice which I should like to turn into a slogan to live by: "Always keep moving forward; you can always turn back." Whether it be ideas, feelings, books, always forward, ahead to something new. The day will perhaps come when we'll be happy to have something to go back to.

I'm so anxious to see you—not because it seems as if it's been too long—you're always close to me. But there are so many things which I can't seem to write, which are constantly on my mind. It seemed easier to write from Finland. I know that talking to you will mean that a lot of new horizons will open up for me.

I probably won't be going to sea for the next few months. This bothers me in a way, but as you can probably imagine, I'm enjoying life at home to the utmost.

ON AUGUST 15, 1942, *Kim enrolled at Ahm for a one-year course intending to obtain a degree which would make him eligible for Naval Officers School. At the same time Hanne left for the country to study home economics.*

After a month at the school Kim was told that he didn't have the slightest chance of getting through and that he might as well give up right away. But Kim was determined. When the examination was announced, only three students out of the class were qualified to take it. Out of the three two passed, and one of them was Kim.

On June 29, 1943, Kim passed his mathematics examination, but his average was too low to enable him to compete with the sixty brilliant candidates who were competing for the thirty places in the Cadet Training School. He returned to the Merchant Marine with what almost amounted to a feeling of relief.

This year of intensive study didn't leave much time for letter-writing.

10 October 1942

Dear Hanne,

Have you ever read *Adam Homo*, about the mother who teaches her little boy the meaning of "to be"? Hanne, I feel more strongly even than before the importance of "to be" for us both. It isn't only that we love each other. It's something more; something much bigger than we are. Some call it nature and some call it God, but you know that for us it's the trees, the birds, the clouds and the two buzzards with their black-on-white effect against the cloud masses. Also it's the fledgling you saw yesterday flying from its nest. It's the excitement we felt when we cut through the fjord under full sail while you were hanging on to the sheet—the sky, the clouds, the cold, clear morning air, the little bird fluttering over our heads—a world which reaches up and beyond, a moment so beautiful that there are no words to describe it. It's nature and much more than nature—one heart that beats in unison with another, close to nature, under the open sky. This is probably the most beautiful, the most sublime of all the things that we are stumbling around in search of.

AT SEA 5

1 August 1943

Have signed on a three-masted schooner *Erna of Marsal* as ordinary seaman.

A new chapter in my life is beginning. I do hope that it is a good one and that I will be alert and awake enough to take advantage of every opportunity that comes my way to learn.

EN ROUTE TO KORSOER
2 August 1943

Dearest Hanne,

I'm sitting on my suitcase in a crowded train as I write this, feeling very sleepy. Two people in love are standing beside me. The man just gave me a long, black look as if he were accusing me of disapproving of them. Idiots! They ought to be making better use of their time than trying to justify themselves.

Now I'm on board the ferry. There's a girl standing beside me—cute, of course; otherwise I wouldn't be standing here, would I? She looked at me and I smiled back, and now I catch her eye every time I look up. Will I be able to resist, Hanne? You'll vouch for me, won't you? People are the most fascinating creatures to watch. She is glancing through a newspaper; now she turns a page. Her face has the expression that you often see on people's faces when they withdraw from their surroundings and absorb themselves in their papers.

I'm leaning against the railing right by the stairs looking at people and having a wonderful time. You know how pleasant a trip can be if you're in the right mood—every little thing attracts your attention. If you were only here!

A couple of rowboats are going by. They look so small from here; they seem to belong to a different world—two small worlds afloat in the same sea. Doesn't the same feeling exist between nations, between races and between neighbors and families? Every group forms its own little world—millions of little worlds floating around in the big world, all with the feeling that they are sufficient unto themselves. But they lack the vision to fill their worlds. If this vision isn't inherited, can't it be acquired by education? Through education comes wisdom and through wisdom, understanding.

MARSTAL
3 August 1943

This has been my first day on board. There are eight of us—four in the crew's quarters. There is a deckhouse on this ship. Two of us are ordinary seamen. The other one is a nice guy, calm and steady. Makes a good impression. The two apprentices are real bastards. One is a little operator who has already been to sea for a year, and the other one is a big bully, so lazy he can hardly put one foot in front of the other. Pretty disgusting characters, both of them. The skipper is a really wonderful guy. He is a big fellow, powerfully built, weighing about two hundred fifty pounds—all muscles. The ship isn't rigged yet, so it will be a few days before we are ready to sail.

Today I suddenly had the feeling that I wouldn't be able to lead this kind of life for too long. Don't think it's because I don't like the life at sea or that it's because I miss you so terribly much. These aren't the reasons. It's only that I have such an urge to be able to read and to have as much time for reading as I had before I signed on this ship.

I've been ashore a few times with my mate. All he does when he goes into town is to walk up and down the main drag saying hi to everybody. Once in a while he bent down and picked up cigar and cigarette butts. He even picked up a butt, sopping wet from the rain, pressed the water out with his fingers and put it in his pocket. When we got back to the ship he turned his pockets inside out and filled his pipe with its contents.

We can hear the bombing in Germany.

MARSTAL

4 August 1943

I'm surprised how pleasant it is not to be an apprentice any longer. If I'm stuck with a nasty job, I just grab one of those fellows by the scruff of the neck and . . . Today I threw one of the apprentices out of his bunk and took it over myself. It's so much better than mine. I hesitated at first because I didn't want to start any trouble on board, but today I felt so cocky that I decided to appropriate it after all. We made a short run to adjust the compass and tomorrow morning at 4 o'clock we sail.

5 August 1943

I'm now on the bridge with a smoky lamp beside me. The whole ship is sleeping. I'm the only one awake, watching over everything like an almighty father and making sure that all is in order. We are lying at anchor and the ship is rocking in the gentle swell left by yesterday's gale.

I'm sitting here leaning my head on my hand, the writing pad on my knees. I've planted both feet on the wheel. The door is open and from it leads a path of the purest silver. The full moon out there beams on the water and the ship. It's this path my thoughts take to go in search of Hanne, my fairy queen.

Like a moonbeam I imperceptibly steal into your room. You don't see me because your lamp is lit and I'm too weak to shine through its glow. Almost invisible, I spread myself out at the foot of your bed. Oh, if I only weren't so far away! If only I were bright enough to outshine your lamp and attract your attention. Slowly, very slowly, I glide up over your covers. You are writing, leaning on your elbow. Your pen stops moving and your eyes have a faraway look. Hanne, Hanne, look at me! I'm here. Darling, look at me only once! But no, you make a slight movement and start writing again. I glide a little closer and am almost obliterated by the light of your lamp, but I don't notice it because everything in me reaches out to absorb what is you in the secure and warm atmosphere of your home and the quiet calm you radiate.

Now you are wandering off into a dream again. You close your book and put it away; you get up to pull the curtains aside. Your eyes are misty as you stand there looking out into the endless distance in search of me. But Hanne, look at me. I'm here with you. Your thoughts needn't wander around the universe in search of mine because I'm right here with you. Now you're slowly walking away, and now I can rest on your covers. This moment is so perfect, so still, that if I weren't a moonbeam I could cry. I move up over your covers and for a moment I caress your face. Your lips move slightly. Then you turn your back on me and I am left there, disappointed, on the edge of the bed. Then I glide down on the floor, meet up with a pair of slippers and am thrilled at the thought that they belong to you. I linger by them for a second and then softly steal away the way I came, disappearing with the dawn. Forgive me, my love, if I disturbed you and your sleep was troubled.

The sun is steadily climbing and in the east the sky is a riot of color. The air is feather-light and pure but the earth is still enveloped in dusk. I'm standing at the railing to greet the dawn of this new day, not making a move for fear I will disturb this heavenly peace which prevails.

6 August 1943

They woke us up at 4 o'clock this morning and we had a good trip through the straits. But then we got into a storm and had to reef our sails. We also had engine trouble and had to go in to Kerteminde where we are at present.

Something funny happened to me tonight. I told Jens to wash the forecastle. He refused, but I didn't slap him. I don't know myself any more, but I just can't make myself strike anyone.

5 September 1943

Have been to Copenhagen, Stettin, and back to Copenhagen again Saturday, Sunday and most of the week because of a fire which broke out in the hold. Witnessed the taking over of the Danish government by the Germans. Back in Stettin. Have talked with some of the dockworkers. They are all French, Belgian and Russian prisoners of war. The French especially are in bad shape. They seem to have lost all desire to live. They see nothing, say nothing, and what's more, do nothing. One of them told me that he went into a shop and was told, "Foreigner, get out."

While we were sitting around in the crew's quarters yesterday, there was a knock at the door. I called out, "Come in"; whereupon the door opened and a little man stepped from the darkness outside into the light. I thought he looked like a bookbinder or a carpenter. (He turned out to be the latter.) He came in with his hat in his hand, and timidly pleaded for bread. Durant didn't eat anything but gave the little man his share. The man asked if he couldn't buy a shirt, and Durant gave him one of his.

HELLERUP
4 December 1943

My dear Nitte,

I don't know if you've already heard that I've been discharged. I came home a week ago with a bad knee. Nothing serious, but the doctor felt that I ought to stay off it for a couple of weeks.

I remember our talking about this once before: that our pride makes us think our physique can endure just about everything. This gives us a feeling of confidence which only those can understand who have had the experience. One thing after another has made me more receptive to new impressions than I used to be and this is a great new gift for which I'm very grateful. But sometimes I'm overwhelmed by a feeling of utter stupidity and confusion which I've never had before. There is also something else that I've wanted to talk to you about for a long time. For the past few years—all my life, in fact—I've somehow felt that I was different from others. In the beginning this feeling was probably only in my subconscious but recently it has grown and developed. I must admit that I haven't tried to repress it. It's such a good prop for my vanity to feel that I'm different. I've tried to understand why this should be, but I've noticed several times that when the odds are really stacked against me this feeling comes out most strongly.

With this gnawing away at me, the first thing I asked myself was what I thought this might lead to. Naturally my first thought was to write, and it still is, but somehow I feel that I don't have what it takes, that I lack the talent. The explanation closest at hand—and perhaps also the right one—is that I was born lucky and that is perhaps why all kinds of thoughts, big and little, keep coming and going in my head concerning myself.

Perhaps you'll be surprised by all this, and maybe some day I'll laugh at it all myself and put it out of my mind. And yet

—I wonder if that is possible. But you know how a thought changes the moment it ceases to be an idle fancy in our minds and takes form on paper. Affectionate regards.

I have let this letter lie around for a couple of days on purpose and, honestly, I have a good mind not to send it at all. But you probably realize that so much is going on in my mind at the moment that it's impossible to try to analyze it, much less try to explain it. Nevertheless it sometimes seems to help. I'm sure this looks as if I'm taking myself too seriously, but it isn't that.

Let me try to explain what I mean. Do you remember the time we went skiing by moonlight? The atmosphere of the moment which meant such an awful lot to me would seem flat and dull if I were to try to explain it to you. Yet I know that you would understand something of what I felt because you were there and perhaps even lived that moment the same way I did. You have probably gone through this and that is why I want to share my most recent experiences with you. I feel as if I were being tossed around by a big wave which washes over me and sucks me down.

CALLISENVEJ, HELLERUP
18 December 1943

My dear Nitte,

Here we're back again to the traditional Christmas letter with all the old hand-me-down phrases so lacking in the warmth they ought to convey.

I've been reckless enough to start this letter in the morning. I don't know why, but I'm always ill at ease when I have to write in the morning. I painfully pull sentence after sentence out of my numb brain and I don't feel any of the energy which carries me forward when I pick up my pen late at night.

I've often thought of your great admiration for the Bible,

your love for it and for Jesus, or to say more precisely what I mean, your love of an ideal which you have gradually created in your mind, an image which life and experience will enrich and widen for you and which will fill you more and more as time goes by. But I know that you will never reach the stage where you worship the image which you yourself have created, as so many people do who find themselves carried along on a wave of faith. They close their eyes in silent prayer and blind submission without trying to look down into the depths of their souls. I said "image" on purpose because I know the love and appreciation you feel for a real work of art, and I have the feeling that your mind has created a beautiful statue into which you have breathed life and which has been molded by all the impressions you have gathered along your way from books, from the Bible and from your own mind. All this has formed into one beautiful creation. Every time you open this book of books you discover more things about yourself, and this fills you with a great sense of happiness. And so the statue keeps on growing—or is it your mind? You're not quite aware of it yourself, but you do know that something is constantly being created in you, something which must be held high above the frustrations of everyday life from which it is so hard to free ourselves.

In your heart you cherish this effigy, but you are not bound by it because with adoration the mind begins to close so that you can't see or feel or hear anything. I can't imagine your being blinded by devotion, unable to see all the beauty which life has to offer. You feel that man would rather renounce this priceless gift of freedom to think, and give himself up in dutiful prayer and admiration—that he would rather have an angel to look up to.

But you feel in your heart, despite the security which an image gives, a strong urge to be your own god—a free spirit with a profound respect and love for the life you yourself have created.

I don't know if you remember that I once asked you if I could freely write you everything which came to my mind. You immediately answered yes in such a matter-of-fact way that I was quite surprised because I know your dislike of anything that seems like indiscretion. I wonder if you realized what a shock you might be exposing yourself to. Perhaps you did know, but as you said at the time, this was something on which we did not see eye to eye. But the fact that I asked this of you proves my confidence in you to a far greater extent than you could possibly imagine.

I just got your wrist watch. Thanks ever so much. You may not believe it, but I was even more happy to receive your letters. You mention that the strap cuts into the wrist. You know how a sudden flash of a thought can make you feel warm all over? I can see you now with my watch on your wrist and I'm happy over this most recent link between us.

TRELLEBORG
8 January 1944

Dearest Hanne,

We've had bad weather and had to take refuge here. Went up to have a look around the town and was annoyed to find that all the shops were closed. There were so many things I wanted to buy, since we'll be taking off early tomorrow morning. The Swedes show a great interest in our plight and even the man in the street is upset about the murder of Kaj Munk.[1] Funny, how superior we feel to them because we're taking part in this fight whereas they are only sitting on the sidelines. They take in everything we say, and it's easy to see how eager

[1] Danish clergyman-playwright, famous during the German occupation for his courage and ideas.

they are to pick up some information that they can pass on. But we're very cautious.

ROENNE
11 January 1944

Left Trelleborg at 10 o'clock last night and arrived here at 8 this morning. The weather was terrible. Our main mast broke. The *Erna* is also here and I went over and paid them a visit. Everything was the same—just as filthy as ever. The crew's quarters were darker and more miserable than I remembered them. When I lived in the midst of it, I sort of got to like it in spite of everything and didn't notice how dingy it was until just now.

ROENNE
13 January 1944

We have now finished our unloading and have begun to load pottery for Randers. Today I bought a map of Bornholm, and since we're staying here over Sunday I thought I'd visit the interesting places in the vicinity.

Funny how easy it is to put an idea across on board here. I'm sure the cook hasn't washed since he's been on this ship, and now he seems to take a delight in being clean. I can't help laughing when I see how he prances about admiring himself. We've scrubbed the crew's quarters clean and have finally got down to the bottom layer of the dirt, and oh how good it feels!

ROENNE

14 January 1944

Today we loaded an enormous amount of bricks. We figured out that each of us had handled forty tons of bricks on the way to the hold today. It was backbreaking work, especially since we aren't used to it.

While I was operating the winch, an old man came to have a word with his son, a driver of one of the trucks. I couldn't help watching them—the old fellow and the young one. There was something about the old man's face; the network of fine wrinkles was like a frame around the calm, blue eyes. They were so wise, and for the first time I really understood the difference between youth and age. He reminded me of Grandfather. These wise old men with a world of insight and moral strength—when you see them walk, stiff and bent, you feel an affection well up inside you for them, although at the same time you brace your shoulders, secure in the thought that you are young and strong.

ROENNE

16 January 1944

I've been watching a rock which protrudes slightly over the water level. The sea slowly backed away from it and then playfully covered it again. Suddenly I saw something new in the drawings of Leonardo da Vinci. I had never really understood his drawings of waves before, but all at once they became alive to me. In another place the water had drilled a hole into the cliff, behind which a little lake had formed. I watched the calm surface rise and sink, in perfect rhythm with its mother, the sea.

As I walked by a church I heard people singing psalms inside, and when they had stopped I went in to look around. The pastor shook hands with me and said it was a pity I hadn't come an hour earlier. On one of the walls hung a large portrait of my paternal grandfather. I asked if the vicarage was still standing, but the pastor told me that it had been completely destroyed by fire. When he heard that I was the grandchild of the former pastor, he told me to go and talk to Martine Mortensen, an old lady who would be happy to see me. She was a tailor's widow and over eighty years old. She lived quietly and peacefully for her God, her fellow men and her memories.

I greet her and am at once admitted into her world of the past. She smiles as she clears off the table, and her smile is the serene, gentle smile of the very old and the very young. I already feel a great fondness for her. She reminisces about something and is carried far away by her thoughts. Then she smiles again. When she smiles she is childlike, and when she sinks into thought I see experience and suffering in the million tiny wrinkles in her face. She talks about Grandfather and Grandmother, and how hard Grandfather worked for the community, and how difficult it was for Grandmother to stand by and watch him killing himself without daring to interfere with the work to which he had dedicated himself.

As the old woman talked, I could see before me the beautiful young parson's wife with her nine small children, struggling to make ends meet on their meager earnings. And I could see the tall, handsome pastor who is always inviting people home for meals, always working, sometimes not even allowing himself time to eat. Always in the background is this brave little woman, probably a little sad because her husband has so little time for anything but his work. But she is always there ready with her help and support.

"Your grandfather saw the meaning and value of every little

thing and knew how to interpret all this to others." I was delighted to hear her put it this way. Then she talked about herself and she smiled and said proudly, "My husband and I have always been very poor, but honest, and we have never caused anyone to suffer." Then a cloud passed over her face as she added, "We had to skimp on food and clothing to make it go around. To make it go around," she repeated, and fell into thought.

The pious old lady was sad because I had been on the road while the church sermon was going on. But she smiled her wise old smile and said, "But to be alone out in the open is also a form of prayer." Then she took me out to a small, scrubby garden. "You should have seen how beautiful this was in the summertime," she said. Like a blind man to whom something is being described, I had some difficulty in imagining this. She pointed to an old, gnarled pear tree. I couldn't see anything special about it, but then the secret of the tree came out. "My husband planted it." And she added, "I like to watch it grow." We made a tour around the garden, and believe me, this little patch held more secrets and fond memories than an old estate. Every stone had a meaning for her, and the old woman laughed happily like a child showing off its treasures. But soon again she was deep in thought.

We walked back to her little house. In her room were two beds, and she wanted me to be sure to remember that one of them would always be at my disposal. I was deeply moved and thanked her with all my heart.

She told me what Grandfather had said when she and her future husband had come to him to arrange for their marriage. The man was deaf, and my Grandfather had pointed out that life wouldn't be easy for them. They had both looked down for a moment, but then the man had raised his eyes, looked at her and said, "Yes, but we love each other so much." Then the pastor had smiled at them and said that if that were the case all would be well.

She was quiet for a moment, and then she looked out of the window and said, "When they're gone, they're really gone." It was as if she were making a slight reproach to God and her fate, but then she brightened up and said, "Thank God that we have our memories."

Suddenly she folded her hands and started to pray with all the fervor that was in her heart. She prayed for our beloved Denmark, for the Danish seamen, for my family and for me. When she had finished she looked at me with her kind old eyes and said, "Although I'm poor I would so very much like to do something for you."

When I left she squeezed my hand so hard that I was quite taken aback—she almost wouldn't let go. The door got stuck, and she gave it such a jerk that I thought her arm would go out of joint, but she seemed quite used to it.

While walking toward the station I thought of her. Seldom have I been so moved. I thought of the little Christmas tree which was still standing in her little room, and realized that by hanging on to this tree she was trying to hold on to time which was slowly leading her toward death from which there was no appeal. This brought home to me more strongly than ever that every minute ought to be lived as if it were the first and last. Even we who are young are so close to eternity without realizing it. All of our life we're really saying good-bye, but the young live secure in the feeling that all of life lies before them.

GRENAA
29 January 1944

I've had fun watching the fishermen bring their fish to the markets. It's a very dark night and the port is brightly illuminated with gas jets. I lost my pea jacket in Randers. I've been thinking of the big tycoon, P.O., and can't help comparing him to A.H., both out for all they can get. They have that quality which makes the English so strong, but to me they are giving up all that is important in life. They cling to a milestone and don't dare to move ahead for fear of missing what they have already accumulated.

ROENNE
2 February 1944

During the Trelleborg-Roenne run, while I was standing at the helm struggling with a ship that tossed on the waves and a seasickness that did its best to toss everything out of me, I felt happy at the thought of the letters which would perhaps be waiting for me at Roenne.

A human being is made up of so many things which his senses have instilled in him from before he can remember. He has built himself a house—a whole world, in fact, and in this he lives more or less at peace with himself. Then one day he meets up with something which has no place in his world. It may be a thought, a desire or something he has divined in the expression of someone's eyes. A meeting with the unknown would fill an animal with fear; but man, if his spirit is truly alive, will suddenly feel that he has caught a glimpse of eternity, despite all the ties by which he is bound to his own world.

ROENNE
7 February 1944

Yesterday was Sunday, and the cook and I went up to visit Ekkodalen and Rytterknaegten. The fellow turned out to be darned good company. We walked about seven miles along the open road, and then climbed around on the rocks until the sun went down. We ran most of the way back. The weather was magnificent with a sprinkling of frost over a thin layer of snow. We looked just like two tramps: a tall fellow and a short one; one with a long beard and the other one pretty grimy; both with patched jackets, upturned collars and noses blue from cold. When we came back on the road and had walked for about five minutes, the cook started to look all around him and came out with: "I wonder if there isn't a baker around?" Then two minutes later: "I'll die if I don't get to a baker soon." We met a young couple and took them by surprise just as he was about to wash her face with snow. She smiled gaily while the man gave us a black look. The cook kept on complaining about how hungry he was and how terrible it was that he couldn't find a baker. We ended up by ordering two plates of hash at the hotel by the railway station in Aakirkeby. He had his eye on an ash tray and saltcellar that he wanted to pinch, but when the waitress came to serve us he forgot all about it and settled down to pick his nose and stare at her.

SOENDERBORG
17 February 1944

How wonderful life is if you want to live it to the full! A boy and a girl run along the shore holding hands. They are laughing and singing and everything is pure delight in their world. There are times when they feel that they can rise above everything around them. They are so far up in the clouds that no one can reach them, or even judge them.

You and I will live our lives in such a way that we will be able to look back without regrets. Being afraid to look back means that life was squandered and that its wonderful essence ran out in the sands. When we're young and strong it's the moment and the future that count and the memories accumulate as a reserve fund. We speed ahead, right into the arms of death, but without fear because there is nothing we would have wished to be different.

Don't be worried because you don't know what you will do when you graduate from the Academy. Just keep steadily moving forward with your eyes open, so that you won't miss any of the little miracles unfolding before you. Look over there! At the side of the road is a little house so lovely that you just have to go in. You feel that you have to explore it and get to know it. You knock at the door and your heart beats faster as you wait. The door opens and an old man stands before you with a friendly smile. You haven't been inside for more than five minutes before you feel as if you had known it all your life and as if you had always lived there. I hear your voice and your laughter inside this house, which is unknown to me.

Hanne, if you're walking down the road it would be foolish to worry about whether you are going to find a house which corresponds to your dreams. If you go for a walk, you usually go to explore and to take in what is around you and make discoveries. Keep on going, and when the time comes, we'll see if the house which you've dreamed about isn't just around the last bend of the road.

MOMMARK

19 February 1944

Today I jammed the middle finger of my left hand and it throbs and burns like blazes. I've tried to read. No dice. It seems as if all my faculties were concentrated in the tip of the throbbing finger. The hatch cover fell on it, but at the time my hands were cold and I didn't feel the pain. But when

I got down to the warm cabin it really started to hurt, and when I dipped it in warm water I almost went through the ceiling. Since then I've been pacing the floor the way you do when the pain is unbearable. Now I'm in my bunk. The other boys are asleep. I'm gritting my teeth. I have the radio and the light on, but no matter how I try, I can't seem to get away from my blue finger. I twist and turn and try to write to pass the time, but nothing helps.

MOMMARK
20 February 1944

Your voice on the telephone! I can hardly believe that it's only a half-hour since I heard your voice. I really called to congratulate my little sister on her birthday. I was also hoping to be able to say a few words to you. It was getting dark. I went to the pay station but there wasn't a soul around. I fumbled around trying to find the receiver, but instead I got hold of the blackout curtain and it flew up. The telephone turned out to be locked. Then I walked out in the country, went into a barn and asked one of the men who was working there if I could use the phone. He took me over to the main building, where I knocked at the door, knocked again, and finally a young woman opened up. I told her what I wanted and she brought me into the dining room. There was no one around but the table was set for three. I put in my call and sat down to wait. If I had only known what was in store for me!

Until then I'd been quite calm. After an endless time Ruth came to the phone. I had no idea what to say to her. Then I asked for Hanne, and there you were at the other end of the line, holding the receiver with the whole family standing around gaping at you. That's more than a little girl can bear.

In order to hide your emotions you talked for their benefit —and not for mine. At the other end of the phone was another imbecile talking from a farm and he too had only one idea in his head: to get away as fast as possible. I was such a lamebrain, for when you tried to get us out of this by asking me if I didn't want to talk to Ruth again, I asked if all you could think about was to get away. My little darling, I didn't want to make it worse for you; I was just teasing. Still I was quite calm. I paid, excused myself for having disturbed the people, and left. The woman very kindly turned the lights on and showed me out and there I was in the inky blackness on a remote Danish farm, still with the echo of your anxious little voice in my ears.

Maybe you'll understand why I ran the two miles back to the ship without stopping.

EN ROUTE FROM
SVENDBORG TO RANDERS
24 February 1944

We left this morning and arrived at Svendborg around noon. Went to have a talk with the shipowner about an order he issued to the effect that we were to do extra watches without overtime.

He was sitting at his desk with his attorney standing at his side as we came into his office. I told him our errand. He reached for the regulations governing pay which he so conveniently had lying on his desk, and read a passage from it out loud proving that he was justified in making this demand. Then he explained how necessary it was to guard against theft, etc. I answered politely that we understood this perfectly, but that we also had the right to ask more pay for more work. Yes, but it wasn't possible for them to raise our pay since it might establish a precedent. At that moment the phone rang. Yesterday *Lenskov* hit a mine near Femern. "Luckily the crew was saved, but it was exasperating because the war risk insurance on this ship wasn't very high." The order of importance of these two things in his mind was quite obvious. In the end he offered us five crowns more per month. [one dollar]

6 March 1944

Monday morning outside Travemünde. Calm, moonlight. One day the cook decided that he would like to write a page in my diary. Since he and Mogens had already told me of their first impressions of me, I took him up on it and this was the result:

> We had to replace a seaman in Randers. We're always curious to see what sort of a mate we're getting. The skipper told us that he would be coming tonight. I was standing around the crew's quarters with my mates. Then we saw a pair of such big feet and such long legs that we couldn't believe what we saw. Our quarters are big but not big enough for him. I only reach up to his armpits when I stand on tiptoe.
>
> The first few days we sort of kept watching him from a distance. He looked like a queer sort of fish. My mate and I kept hoping that he'd go back where he came from because it was impossible to keep a giant like that on board. But when we had worked with him for a couple of weeks we changed our minds. We've started to talk to him now and we think that given time he might turn out to be O.K. and become a smart fellow someday.
>
> In remembrance of your old shipmate, Fanoe.
>
> P.S. Think about what you'll be like when you hit fifty.

LÜBECK
7 March 1944

Tonight I went ashore for a while. On the pier was a big heap of all the private planes which the Germans have stolen at Kastrup Airport. It was sickening to see what they had done to them. They only want the parts and don't give a hoot about the planes, and so they had thrown them there in a pile as if they were a load of coal, and there they were, still flying their small Danish flags, which seemed to be calling out to us.

Today I was talking to some Germans. The first one was a big and important-looking foreman, a little less repulsive than most Germans with their steely blue eyes which are a camouflage for their stupidity. He was arrogant as most Germans are and so aggressive that I was disgusted, but the other fellows didn't feel quite the same way I did. He came down to give us a message while we were having coffee. He asked if there was any more coffee and the reply was typically Danish: "Oh, what the hell, give him a cup." When he had finished his coffee, he went over to the table and buttered himself not one but two pieces of bread. I said slowly and with great emphasis that it wouldn't be long now before he would be sent to work in Russia. He was getting madder by the minute, but I have to say to his credit that he shot me a warning look when he noticed an officer standing a few paces from us.

The next one I talked to was a German soldier. A Russian came toward him and I saw that the German's face had a friendly expression. They talked and it turned out that the soldier had been a prisoner in Russia during the last war and that he had been well-treated. The Russian was hungry. He pointed to his stomach and looked at us with his slanting, brown eyes which seemed so expressionless to me. Mogens went down and got half a loaf of rye bread and a quarter of a pound of butter. The soldier looked at the Russian, smiled and said, "Now you're a millionaire." The strange face lit up with pleasure. I suddenly felt a warm wave of affection for this odd-looking fellow who had been a stranger to me just a few seconds ago. At this moment I happened to glance at the foreman. He gave a fatherly smile of approval when the Russian got the bread, but when he saw the butter his eyes turned ugly with envy. Oh, you supermen of the master race who can stoop so low for a quarter of a pound of butter!

Later on while I was talking to the soldier, the next guard down the line suddenly called out, "Enemy approaching." Astonished, I asked if the English were coming, although I knew that no alert had been sounded. He smiled and shook his head. "The Gestapo," he said.

He was a nice fellow, that soldier, thin and haggard-looking with kind eyes and a gentle manner. When I was going ashore the only thing he said was, "Pass, please" and his eyes looked beyond me which clearly indicated that he had no intention of examining my pass closely. He was convinced that Germany would win the war, but when we had proved to him that Germany had already been defeated, he smiled and seemed to dismiss the argument from his mind. He believed that England was through, and he illustrated this with a gesture of his hand showing that the Germans would make a large hole where England is and that England would disappear in this hole.

Tonight I've been talking to an Austrian saloon-keeper. He was burning up with hatred for the Germans. He put his face close to mine and the whites of his eyes showed as he gave vent to all his indignation. He trembled with rage and seemed for once to be able to let himself go. But it was quite a shock to see how humble he became when another guard passed by.

The town is covered with posters—all telling the same story.

One depicts a railway station crowded with happy Germans, taken from above. Over the picture lies the heavy shadow of a man in a big coat, and underneath is printed in large letters: "The enemy is listening." Two of the posters preach economy, and I'll never be able to forget the last one. It shows an ugly face reflected in a hand mirror, looking very much like a rat and with a loathsome expression over his features. Almost in relief is an angular, semitic nose and the caption under the poster reads: "Look at yourself in the mirror. Are you a Jew or aren't you?" How rotten all of these people must be in order not to react violently to this. The Germans are like a ripe fruit that has been damaged and now the rottenness has come to the surface.

DIDIER FACTORY, STETTIN
11 April 1944

We came into the free port and lay at anchor there for a day, after which we shifted over here. Since then so many things have happened that I couldn't even begin to tell you about them. If it were at all possible, I would have to begin by painting word pictures of Russians, Poles, French and Germans. I would have to describe the atmosphere in a work camp and how it feels to stand in a line-up of Russians and pretend to be one of them, and how it feels to hide under the bed in one of these camps when the German guard walks by; what it's like to sit with a group of prisoners, watch their dances and listen to their songs and duck your head between your knees and pretend to be a Russian when the guard comes; to see the bombs fall on the town, leaving hollow ruins in its wake; to see the Russians emerge from one of these holes only to disappear again with a new explosion; to walk about in the emptiness of a bombed church among the fragments of what were beautiful stained-glass windows not so long ago; to turn the pages of a psalm book; to be in an empty space which was once a room, with fifty Poles, and at once see a face which draws your attention away from everything else. We talk about Jesus, Socrates, about the Germans and the Russians, and we see the Russians being beaten by an iron bar a yard long.

SVINEMÜNDE
12 April 1944

I've met a Polish student and was amazed to find how much we had in common. As I talked to him I couldn't help feeling that small nations can perhaps justify their existence by being more impartial and more analytical when it comes to political questions. Every night I went to see the Polish boy in a room he shared with thirty other people. It reminded me of the casemates at Kronborg, the only difference being that there was a bright electric bulb in the ceiling.

But to start at the beginning. On Saturday we went through all four bridges and passed through Stettin in beautiful sunshine. Spring was in the air. We were standing around watching the changing scene glide by. Only a wall remained of what must once have been a big building. Beside us were two buoys, both with the word WRECK written on them. Seemed strange, a wreck right in the port. A streetcar disappeared behind a heap of rubble. A curtain fluttered out through a hole in the wall. We had to wait a long time to get through the railway bridge. The sun was boiling hot. I was lazily stretched out on the hatch cover. In one place the house had almost fallen into the harbor. You could still see the light blue, flowered wallpaper. This town is so full of beautiful monuments and churches.

Suddenly we made a turn and headed for something that

looked more like a ditch than a canal. It was just about wide enough to let us through. At the other end of the canal was a big square where the Didier factory was located. Ruins were all that was left of it. We were to pick up a load of bricks and there weren't even enough to make a full load. On the south side of the canal, standing between masses of rubble, was a big machine shop. On the north side was another one, partly in ruins. I had been there a few days before and discovered that it wasn't abandoned.

On the morning of Easter Sunday when I took a walk around the factory, I saw a small square marked off by barbed wire. It looked like a dog kennel and in it were a group of Russian P.W.'s washing their miserable rags. I went over and talked to them and they immediately put their hands through the barbed wire to shake hands. I liked them and felt sorry for them. I got a sweater and some socks and gave them to a big pleasant-looking fellow who seemed to be the leader. He was strong as an ox but in every other respect he seemed like a child. He was delighted with what I had given him and ten minutes later I saw him proudly parading around the enclosure wearing my socks. But I'm sure that the novelty had worn off after a quarter of an hour.

That afternoon the cook and I sneaked ourselves in among the P.W.'s and managed to get into their quarters. There was a ladder outside, resembling a fire escape, which led to the machine shop. This is where the men lived in three rooms, thirty to forty in a room. It looked just like a stable. They had built the bunks themselves, one above the other. There were no mattresses, but wood shavings and two blankets for each. The food consisted of two loaves of rye bread a week (German bread isn't nourishing), less than a pound of margarine per month, a pound of potatoes a day, a pound of sugar a month, and a little cabbage—nothing else. Once in a while they would get some fish but the last time was two months ago. I couldn't understand how they could get by on this, but then it came out that they also had some oil which they stole in a factory where some of them were working. All of them were chewing on sunflower seeds which were used in the making of oil. I couldn't get over how eager they were to be hospitable. The big fellow offered us beer (of this they were given all they could drink).

Among them were boys fourteen to fifteen years of age who had been taken prisoners in the Ukraine for forced labor camps. Ten of them lived in a little house which looked like a small farm laundry at home. I went in and started a conversation with them. After an hour, when they started to eat, I got up to go. One of them with intense blue eyes asked me to sit down again. Surprised, I asked him why, whereupon he lowered his eyes and looked a little embarrassed. "Because you're one of us," he said, and slipped a bottle of oil into my pocket which I just couldn't refuse. I sat down on some rubble and they formed a circle around me. One of them came forward with a banjo with two strings missing, but in spite of this handicap he played extremely well. Their voices when they sang were rich and clear. The little fellow who played was sort of fierce-looking and the others had the greatest respect for him. He was skinny but carried himself well; his face had a harassed and worn look, but I did make him smile once.

Then the fellow standing beside me moved back, leaving a small open space, and here the others started to do their Russian dances for me. One of them did a sort of introductory dance and then stopped in front of one of the other members of the group inviting him to continue. The man who was chosen seemed a bit ill at ease but couldn't refuse. He slowly walked to the center of the circle with his thumbs in his pockets and started to dance a bit awkwardly. But he quickly got into the spirit of the thing, clapping his hands, his face all flushed. When he had finished, the introductory dance was done again and another fellow came out. The big fellow also danced. At first he didn't want to, but then the banjo player clapped his hands and Ivan, this big hulk of a fellow, began to spin around with his arms outspread. Then the dance began and this clumsy-looking guy had suddenly turned into a steel spring.

What fun it would be if we had dances like that. It's a wonderful way of having everyone take part in the general entertainment, and also the performers aren't exposed to the criticism of the passive ones who sit on the sidelines and make remarks.

During the days we spent with them, they were singing and dancing all the time. Once while the cook and I were sitting around with them, someone came in to warn us that the guard was on his way and we had a chance to hide ourselves among the others. The boys had got orders to go down to try to raise a ship that was sinking (this was Easter morning) and we sneaked out with them without being noticed. Ivan went behind the ruins to see the ten boys from the Ukraine whom I've already mentioned. There a woman was waiting for him. "This is strictly forbidden." Suddenly I saw the guard come running, stiffly, like a wooden soldier. He had seen Ivan. "Come here, you," he roared. But Ivan, not aware that he had been seen, ducked down among the ruins and ran off to join his comrades. The German came running after him, caught up with him and hit him square in the face with his fists. "What were you doing there?" he shouted and kept on hitting Ivan, who tried as best as he could to defend himself with his hands. The German got more and more excited. Suddenly he leaned forward, grabbed a crowbar and began to thrash the poor fellow. I was afraid he would kill him. It was more than we could stand. We threw ourselves between them. The German used the foulest language but began to waver and became less sure of himself. Afterwards I saw him take out a pocket mirror, carefully comb his hair and go on his way.

15 April 1944

Later on, the cook and I went for a walk through the town. We were both wearing our work clothes and I had my straw shoes on. On our way back a German guard stopped us and asked us what we thought we were doing walking around the town in this getup. I didn't answer, but pulled out my pass as if I hadn't understood him. When we got back to the camp a crowd of the Russian boys were standing around. The dog belonging to the guard followed us, wagging his tail in a friendly way. One of the Russians brutally grabbed the dog by the tail and threw him up in the air before we realized what he was doing. Another fellow kicked the poor beast as he came down. When I asked why, I couldn't get a better explanation than that "He belongs to the German sergeant."

I've been walking around town. A large part of it is just rubble. It seemed so strange to be sitting on a bench in the bright hot sunshine and not to be able to see the passing streetcar for a wall of debris. Two couples came and sat down on the bench. As I sat there watching them, I realized how the man-woman relationship in Germany has deteriorated through the "breeding" propaganda which was launched by Hitler. I thought about the Polish student and the conversation we'd had about women. He—and obviously the upper classes in Poland—have a romantic attitude toward women. We agreed that the German treatment of women and their ideas of the role of women were disgusting. He told of a few instances he had seen. One of the German workers' wives came by every day at lunch time and the other Germans stood around and, to put it bluntly, took a leak wherever they happened to be, without considering her in the slightest. Another of his observations was: "Here in Germany you always see signs reading 'Men and Women' while in Poland they read 'Women and Men.'" We also talked about the various nations' attitudes with regard to women. The English regard women as remote creatures, the French as equals, the Americans as companions, and the Germans as breeding animals.

The cook and I took the streetcar back. We stood on the forward platform of the last car and on the back platform of the first car stood two little Hitler Youths about ten years old. As I stood watching them, one of the little fellows clenched his fist at me. When he saw that it only produced a smile on our part, he was completely bewildered. He gave me a black look, but I laughed out loud and that confused him all the more. He lowered his eyes but kept on looking in my direction from time to time. When we got off he pressed his face against the window and furiously shook his little fist at us.

On Wednesday we had our first air raid. It came in the middle of the day. The sun was bright and the sky was dotted with white clouds, with the blue sky showing in between. The alert sounded, and we saw the Russians running off to pick up their few possessions. They came with their blankets and boots and gathered around the entrance to the little mud hut which served as an air raid shelter. We heard the planes overhead. They weren't flying very high. When they got to the center of town they started to spiral upwards in great circles, each plane leaving a trail of smoke in its wake. Finally they reached an altitude where they could no longer be seen, but we saw the parallel lines of smoke which were shooting toward the interior of Germany. All was quiet for about an hour. Then they returned—this time at a height of about two miles—one formation after another in endless succession. The anti-aircraft guns opened fire. I was standing in a big machine shop under which there was a bomb shelter, talking to a little Frenchman with no chin to speak of and a pointed nose, who was studying a French-German dictionary.

The shooting increased in intensity. I went over to the other end of the building to look for the Poles. The shell splinters began to rain down, and we could see the shells exploding between the planes. Suddenly I saw a plane on fire, but it was out in a few seconds. One was shot down, but it was behind a cloud so I didn't see it get hit, nor did I see it go down. But then one of the parallel lines separated itself from the others; it got back into line for a few minutes and then went straight down into the forest, leaving a trail behind it in the sky. At almost the same moment a vertical line shot out from one of the planes—one after another, eight in all. The Germans thought that they were downed planes, but we could distinctly see them continue their flight, and we also caught sight of something which looked like a black dot going down with an insane speed. But we didn't hear a thing, probably because of the roar of gunfire. I thought they were incendiary bombs, but they turned out to be explosive bombs instead.

20 April 1944

From Korsoer I went to Copenhagen for the week-end. Hanne was at the station, absolutely enchanting and so happy to see me again. I'm afraid I was a bit withdrawn; I couldn't get my mind off all the things I'd seen—couldn't seem to free myself from them. Not until Sunday was I myself again and able to open up and respond to her.

RANDERS
23 April 1944

It's funny, but my feeling after our last visit to Germany is something which is more like disappointment than anything else. I was under the impression that we were being confronted by an enemy who was powerful, evil, cruel, without scruples, etc. Instead, everywhere I went I saw only weakness and stupidity. It almost reminds me of hell in *A Soul After Death.* I think there is something to the theory that people end up by resembling the country in which they live. I can't forget the incident about which the Polish student told me one day when he came back from town. The alert had sounded while he was in the streetcar, whereupon a fat woman exclaimed, "What have we done that we and our city should be destroyed?" He looked at her with contempt. "I'm Polish," he said.

LÜBECK
30 April 1944

. . . How I wish that I were wandering around in a faraway and unknown land with no thoughts to weigh me down, wandering over endless steppes, into deep forests and over high mountains in the sun and rain; to be thousands of miles away from people—you and I. We are walking and it's raining. We're soaking wet and we don't own a thing in the world but our high spirits and our good health. We continue our wandering, far from everyone and everything until we're exhausted. Have you ever been on a more wonderful adventure? An adventure full of happy energy, dampness and the sweat of our own toil.

LÜBECK
7 May 1944

We're shoving off tomorrow, so I just wanted to write you a few lines.

Remember the day I came to see you in order to talk over my plans for the future? Suddenly you asked me a leading question: Did I intend to wander around the world as a sort of cross between a vagabond and a roving priest? You hastened to add that it would probably be wiser for me to do my traveling as a seaman, so that my life would have some sort of pattern. But every day my urge to wander around the world barefoot and free as a bird grows stronger.

On the other hand, I realized for the first time today that my love for the sea has now taken root. Before, I loved this kind of life because it satisfied so many things in me. I enjoyed the feeling of freedom and at the same time I felt that I wasn't a slave to the sea. Today I suddenly knew that I'm caught and bound to it by the strongest chains. I felt as if the sea had found a place within me. This was a strange discovery and an alarming one. After being as free as the air, I'm now being pulled down by a wave, farther and farther down until all that is left of me is just a plain seaman. On the sea you're either happy or unhappy. There is no in between, and I'm very happy.

I often read the Bible, and find it fascinating. I'm making some notes which you might be interested to look at sometime. And now good night—and thanks for everything.

We didn't get off after all.

It seems strange to be wandering around here observing the Germans. The other day I was talking to a couple of them and told them what the outlook was. They listened attentively, something which is most unusual, but when the conversation reached a certain point they closed their ears. This was when I tried to explain that Germany was finished, and that the only thing which kept Germany going was that the people still believed in a German victory. I was groping around for their vulnerable spot, and suddenly there it was. "But that is what the English are trying to make us believe," they said. They refuse to believe it or even give it a thought because this is the idea that the British propaganda is trying to impress on them. It's very difficult to make any headway with them when they keep on repeating this. I tried to make them see that the English might be right after all, but they flatly refused to listen to this. They were like animals who smelled a trap and wouldn't let themselves be lured into it. "Russia is done for," they say with conviction, "and we're only waiting for more strikes in England."

One of them told me that his house had been bombed, and ended up, "We Germans have only one mission in life: to fight and to win. Let the English drop all the bombs they want to. We can take it."

I've sent you a pound of tea. Please send half of it on to Mother. I haven't had the time to make up two packages. Do let me know as soon as possible if you like it.

AALBORG
12 May 1944

Dearest Hanne,

Yesterday I saw them carry the corpse of the cabin boy the Germans shot on board the *Dannebrog*. Everyone had been informed of the incident, so all the dockworkers were on hand. His shipmates in their work clothes received the coffin on board. They handled it as they would a sail. Slowly and carefully they secured it to the hatch cover, arranged all the wreaths and flowers around it, and draped it in the Danish flag. There were signs of deep emotion on all the rugged young faces. The Danish ships flew their flags at half-mast, and there was a profound silence everywhere. Around various buildings in port the flags were also at half-mast. It was a deeply moving sight —the grave faces of the dockworkers and the awkward way in which they pulled off their caps when the coffin passed by.

The puffy representatives from the Seamen's Union in town, however, were a disgusting spectacle. They marched along with a Danish flag so obscured by dates and the name and address of the organization that it looked more like a billboard than anything else. They elbowed themselves ahead of the townspeople, so cocksure of their own importance and indispensable presence. Behind them came two flagbearers with two small flagpoles on which the flags were flying at half-mast while the body was being transported on board, and again when it had reached the ship. The flagpoles were about six feet high, and to me it looked ridiculous and completely lacking in taste. Afterwards I saw some overblown matrons elbow their way forward to shake hands with one of these pompous burghers. He smiled importantly and they exchanged a stream of banalities. How I should have liked to have seen this ceremony with only the dockworkers and the seamen present. Their solemn faces and their clasped hands as they walked behind their dead shipmate gave the moment dignity and saved it from looking like a market procession which was the impression created by the others.

Feeling all funny inside, I went back on board ship and watched the schooner slowly make its way from the pier with its flag at half-mast. On the hatch cover you could see the dark outline of the coffin under the canvas.

13 May 1944

Hanne, I wish you would explain something to me. Do you remember once when Ruth went through the railway station at Helsingoer, the Germans were lying all over the floor with their packs so that she was forced to climb over them? They had tugged at her skirts and shouted after her. She was furious, and had to make a dash for the platform. "That I would like to have seen," you exclaimed, with an expression in your eyes very characteristic of the woman in you (both the expression and the remark). A man would never have reacted in this way. I didn't understand it, and that is probably the reason why it comes back to me after so long. I don't know if it's the same with other people, but years later a trivial remark can crop up in my mind and suddenly throw a new light on something. I then see the importance of a few words which had escaped me before, and it dawns on me that the expression means something entirely different from what the words had led me to believe.

AALBORG

15 May 1944

Went to the movies with Berg last night. He was completely plastered. We were sitting up in one of the last rows of the balcony when suddenly he started to grin à propos of nothing at all, and turned to me and said so that you could hear him in the whole house, "Kim, that guy over there must be a VIP. Look at the fancy getup he's wearing." Then he snickered for a bit until he noticed that something was happening on the screen and yelled out, "Turn on the lights so I can see something." Laughs and hisses from the audience. That seemed to encourage him and he shouted in a good-natured way, "Stop laughing at me. Cook, will you give me a bottle of gin when we get back on board?" "I don't have any more," the cook whispered back. "You're a damned liar," Berg shouted. A woman behind us started to protest. Berg turned around and said in his friendliest voice, "Come now, take it easy, Sister." Then the screen caught his attention again.

The advertisements were on and one of them showed a church with four steeples. Loud enough for everyone to hear he counted, "One, two, three, four, five, six steeples." Then he laughed, very pleased with himself, and said, "Kim, isn't it funny? I know that there are only four steeples, but I can still count six." I told him to sit still. "Try to fold your hands and keep your mouth shut." He obediently folded his hands, sat quiet as a mouse and stared into thin air. The movie was called *The Sixth Shot* and as a background for the list of players there was a hand with a revolver which fired one shot after another. At the first shot I noticed that Berg was again all attention, and for a moment he sat staring at it in a funny way. His hair had fallen down over his forehead and his eyes were sort of bleary. Before I could stop him he shouted "Bang" at the top of his lungs. Again he lapsed into silence and I had no way of guessing what he was going to do next. "Bang, Bang, Bang, Bang, Bang," he yelled. When I bawled him out he looked surprised. "Yes, but it said on the screen that there would be six shots."

I finally managed to shut him up but unfortunately the film happened to be Swedish. Berg seems to have the idea that he speaks Swedish very well and this was his big chance. He stood up and shouted, "*Jag älskar dig.*" [I love you.] There was a roar of laughter from the audience. Its timing with the movie made it twice as funny. Then he said, "Kim, if you give me ten crowns [two dollars] I'll go away." I had taken his money away when I caught him amusing himself by throwing coins into the water. I told him that I'd give him three crowns.

He was delighted and tried to throw his arms around me because I was being such a good pal.

I led him out so that he wouldn't cause any more trouble. But at the exit he tore himself away and went stumbling down the center aisle, and with his cap on the back of his head yelled, "Now I'm going to do a somersault for all of you." And so, God help me, I saw his shadow on the screen as he threw himself forward in the dark and as if by a miracle landed on his feet again. He smiled triumphantly. I went back to my seat while he staggered back down the aisle and went and stood by the railing on the balcony.

The movie kept on grinding along and the hero and the heroine were now locked in their first passionate embrace. Berg put his hand out toward the screen as if to stop them and his voice rang out indignantly, "I'm just not going to put up with this."

He got back on board ship around midnight, a sorry sight. He was messing around the deck with a tub of water he had overturned. His knuckles were bleeding—he had been in a fight with some Germans. He was no dancer but in his present state his feet suddenly seemed to have wings and he executed the wildest dances and did the most breakneck acrobatics I've ever seen. He ended up by having an attack of rage during which he tore his jacket to shreds. I was annoyed but it amused the cook no end. During this session he also ripped both legs off our chairs and crawled half way up the ladder and stood there howling like a madman and tearing at his jacket. Then he started gnashing his teeth and, honestly, I've never heard anything like it. He finally calmed down again. I was afraid that he would crawl into his bunk in that filthy state. I told him to stop gnashing his teeth and start to wash himself "just to see if you can do it." "But you didn't wash your legs or your feet," we said when he came running inside.

"Let's see if you can do it when you're in your bunk." But two minutes later he was snoring.

5 June 1944

Left for Naestved on Monday, but *Patricia* didn't get in before Tuesday. The trip to Norway was the most marvelous thing you could imagine, with a calm sea all the way. It was wonderful to be on a decent ship again. We came in to Drammen and stayed over Sunday. Bent, the apprentice, and I went to Oslo together. It looked miserable, and the hold the Germans have on the town is a terrible thing to see. The Norwegians seemed too poor and oppressed and bled white. We had a rough trip back.

DANZIG
26 June 1944

I asked the German foreman, "Will the war be over soon?" "Yes, in two months," he said. "Then Hitler can pick up his brush again and do this." With pantomime brush strokes he went through the motions of a fence painter.

We had a little skirmish on board yesterday. It seems to be an old seaman's tradition that when a seaman first comes on board and is going to sea for the first time he is "inspected." Inspection means that they put him on a table, pull off his pants and smear his penis with whatever happens to be around—tar, soy sauce, mustard, ink, or anything else they happen to have on hand. This brings to mind the initiation ceremonies of primitive tribes when a boy is crossing the threshold from childhood to manhood. Jumbo had often been threatened by Kaj and Bent that he would be inspected but nothing came of it because Madsen and I remained neutral.

When Jumbo came aft, the mate, Mester, Bent, the cook and I were there. The mate suggested the inspection and no sooner had he uttered the words than they had Jumbo down on the bench and were pulling his pants off. The boy looked so desperate that I couldn't help laughing with the rest.

The hilarity of these grown men at seeing the panic of the boy, and their feeling of excitement at being able to overpower him, certainly is queer. The mate was the most eager of them all, and the cook went about it like a man setting out to do a thorough job.

Here is another thing peculiar to seamen; you could probably call it a form of loyalty. The hatred for a skipper can raise a tempest on board. It can be so intense that the boys would like nothing better than to see him disappear over the side of the ship one dark night. But should a charge be made against him which might prove fatal to his career, the boys are quick to put the brakes on the thing and say, "What the hell, he will soon be going back on land anyway."

NORTH OF GREENLAND

28 July 1944

If you live like a primitive man, you also find yourself acquiring many of his instincts. The Old Testament traces the spiritual development of the individual, and documents all the knowledge of the hidden depths of man.

We follow a series of events which is leading to something —an unknown peak, a king, or simply the son of man. The son of God or the son of man—what we call him makes no difference—God or the Divinity, this invisible tapestry which combines all the secrets of humanity into a single prodigy: Man.

As a unifying principle, as a culmination of this development, Jesus came as a clear and pure example of this relation between man and the Divine. He is the son of man because he lives in us and through us. He is a part of us, part of this infinite tapestry. His insight and his inspiration were of an absolute purity, and therefore he knew what he would mean to mankind. He looks at us with eyes that see all, and with infinite gentleness and sincerity says, "I am the son of God." We are awed and a little afraid because this spirit lives with us. It was born with us and has seen the light of day through our eyes for the first time. It moves forward with me, it rises and falls with me, and finally it dies with me.

Do you see now that Jesus is the son of man?

Again I have the feeling that I'm struggling to find the answer before I've solved the problem.

30 July 1944

Madsen has been telling me about the navigator we had along on the first trip. His wife wouldn't tell him that she was pregnant before he had his examination behind him, although she would be in her seventh month before he was through. Madsen seemed to realize what it must mean for a young woman to be alone with all these new feelings and experiences in which the expectant mother lives. You can imagine how hard it must have been for her when she found out that she was expecting a baby—her struggles to adjust herself to the awakening maternal instincts as the baby developed. Just think of how it must have been for her to go about arm in arm with the man who was the cause of this new life without being able to share a single one of all these experiences with him, and to be alone with the secret that under her heart she carried his and her child. A woman probably never feels a greater need for security and peace in the arms of the man who is the creator of all this. Just think of what it must have meant to her the first time she felt life.

1 August 1944

The Finns have a touch of greatness about them somehow. They carry themselves well both physically and spiritually. They face death with stoic calm and courage and nothing can make them falter.

They hate the Germans intensely. You can hear them saying things like: "There is nothing to do but to kill those bastards. When they leave we'll install ourselves at Hangoe and pick them off one by one with our machine guns."

Today when I was talking to a petty officer I said, "You Finns are having a tough time." "Not at all" was his answer. "Now the Russians are getting a good beating from the Finns. The Russians will always be beaten. The Russian is and will always be a Russian." "Yes, but your country is so small compared to Russia."

"But it takes fifty Russians to lick a Finn."

There is a saying among the workers: "We can't win the war but we must win and we will win."

If you ask Finnish soldiers if the Finns will sign a peace treaty, they seem to feel ill at ease. It's rather a touchy subject with them; perhaps they feel that their honor is compromised somehow. When we came into the harbor the skipper asked the pilot, "Will we be able to get out of here before the Russians come?" The pilot turned white and didn't say another word.

It's wonderful to come from Germany and see how well-treated the Russian prisoners of war are in Finland. When you think of the sacrifice it represents for such a small country, it certainly shows a magnificent spirit. The effort for them is so much greater than for the Germans.

VASA
7 August 1944

Tonight the cook and I have been discussing the Germans, and the punishment that ought to be given them. That fellow is really a Dane to be proud of. He was sick at heart at the thought of all the Germans who would be shot. He felt that punishment ought to be given in such a way that they would be fully aware that it was a punishment. He pointed out how futile it would be to shoot them down without reason at the moment when they would be rejoicing at the thought of going home after five years in military service. Who would have the heart to put a gun against his chest and pull the trigger while they're retreating?

I maintained that this is what most people would do, and that I had heard people talk in dead earnest about sterilizing the whole German people. He shook his head sadly and said, "Then we might as well tie a rope around our necks and hang ourselves, because there would be no further reason to live among men."

VASA
8 August 1944

Today the first officer was telling us about a couple on Fyn. The man worked for the gas company, was small and thin, wore gold-rimmed glasses and was obviously sterile. His wife was nineteen to twenty years old. One day the husband came home and found a man in bed with his wife.

He kept his calm and said to the man, "I suppose that you're going to pay me what you owe me. Give me a daler." [about fifty cents] The fellow was so flustered that he obeyed.

Not with a single word did the man reproach his wife, but he continually kept that coin in his hand and toyed with it. A few months later the wife tried to commit suicide by slashing her wrists. She was caught in time and her life was saved. But when she came back home again, he still went on tossing that coin around, and she ended up by jumping out of a third-story window. The autopsy revealed that the woman was carrying the child of the other man. Three months later the husband was married to someone else.

KEMI, FINLAND
10 August 1944

I was operating the winch and in a perfect spot to watch the women who were working in the hold. They were such a friendly and helpful bunch. One of them, a young girl, was full of the devil. She came walking by when Madsen was standing, leaning his elbow on his knee and looking down into the hold. She got behind him and with her hands around his waist gave him a shove forward, and poor Madsen had to struggle frantically to keep his balance. The next minute she was down there working away, having completely forgotten about Madsen. She was always fooling around, but she still worked harder than any of the others. Madsen and I agreed that we would rather have the job of watching over a sack full of fleas than a girl like that.

KEMI
11 August 1944

Dear Nitte,

It's happened to me that I've lived with people for long periods of time and thought I really knew them, and then one day I suddenly realize that I don't know them at all.

You never see the people you love the way they really are. You wrap a veil around them and go on living with them in a daily routine. During the few seconds when they are visible, your mind is distracted by so many outside things which prevent you from seeing them as they really are. The moments when I've felt that all of Hanne was there for me to see, my heart was so filled with happiness that I couldn't really see her.

I've never really "seen" you but I know what you look like. You have revealed a million little fragments of yourself which I've gradually pieced together like a puzzle.

I remember the last time I came to see you. Miksi was sitting next to me and I pulled out a box of matches from my pocket to see what they were called in Finnish. You said to the little fellow, "It would be fun to have a box of Finnish matches." He looked at me in that expressive, quiet, wide-eyed way of children. I stuck the matches back in my pocket again, and thought how much pleasure a child can find in a little thing like that, but the idea of giving them to him never crossed my mind. Isn't it funny?

Then one night I was standing at the helm. The moonlight was so bright that the rigging and masts were outlined in shadows on the deck, and so sharply that you could even see the fibers in the ropes. I was all alone on deck and there wasn't a sound except an indistinct creaking and a faint clucking along the sides of the ship. Toward the north, the sky had a golden glow. I stood absolutely still at the helm. Every once in a while I would give the wheel a slight turn. Suddenly it struck me that I had forgotten something and in the same instant I knew what it was: to give a little boy a box of matches and see his face light up with pleasure. And only after months do I react! I'm slow, but it's strange how I find myself holding on to something until I'm completely freed from it.

HAUKIPUDAS
27 August 1944

Dearest Hanne,

I found myself thinking about the day when we left Horsens on the *Erna*. The *Fanoe* was there. The crew was standing at the gunwale, and the cook was also there with a girl at his side. I think that she had signed on the ship, but in any case it was evident that the two belonged together. They were a unit, so young—hardly twenty—and so proud and confident. The whole world was there only for them. It was wonderful to see this little fellow, bursting with pride because he was standing next to a woman while all the others were alone.

NORTH OF OEREGRUND
4 September 1944

Last night and this morning we had a bad storm and we had to reef the topsail and douse two jibs. Was seasick.

SOUTH OF THE
STOCKHOLM ARCHIPELAGO
7 September 1944

We were anchored a couple of hundred feet from the pier at Nynaeshamn. I was dying to go ashore to buy some of the things I wanted to bring back for Hanne. The first officer told us that we couldn't have shore passes, but if I would give him the money he would ask the skipper to buy some silk stockings, chocolate, etc., as only the skipper could go ashore. I was ripping mad because I knew that it was all his fault. I had talked to the shore patrol myself and they had been quite friendly and said they would get in touch with the skipper. It wasn't hard to guess what had happened. I thought of going ashore anyway, but Madsen talked me out of it. We waited all afternoon and finally around 7 o'clock the skipper showed up and gave orders to weigh anchor.

The first officer brought me some figs and two pairs of silk stockings, quite nice, but there was no chocolate to be found. I hope that Hanne will be pleased with this. I'm starving and dying to eat the figs. (We're on Finnish rations.) But I'm like the fox running through the fields back to his hole with the bird in his mouth. He drools, he's hungry after a day's hunt, but something compels him to keep going without devouring his prey. It isn't love, sentiment or the desire to please you, but something much stronger, which makes me want to put what I have to give at your feet.

It's such a long time since we've seen or heard from each other. You seem so far away from me that now I really have to concentrate to conjure up your image. But the fact that I couldn't recall the color of your eyes after I came to Finland some time ago doesn't mean that my feelings for you have changed in the least. The love which was awakened in me has grown, but I couldn't say whether the girl in question had blue or brown eyes. I was sure that yours were brown, but was afraid you'd be offended if I wrote and asked you to confirm it! You once wrote and asked me if I could evoke your image without any trouble, and I was scared into telling you a big lie.

JUST NORTH OF GOTLAND
9 September 1944

I'm following the happenings with great suspense. It looks as if a storm were gathering over our little country. It gives me a funny feeling in the pit of my stomach to think that in a few days we may be in the middle of this struggle.

The end is almost in sight, and looking back on the past few years, I wonder whether I have gotten all I could out of them. Have I really made the most out of this crucial time? I've seen a lot which has probably taught me more about life than I would have been able to learn under normal circumstances.

12 September 1944

We ran out of fuel, so had to go to Roenne. We went ashore and I noticed people were staring at me. Beside all these clean and spiffy fellows I realized that I must look like a wild beast from the jungle. I had no sooner gotten ashore than a couple of guys wanted to know what nationality I was. "Canadian? Oh," and they smiled indulgently.

We've all been in high spirits around here. I didn't quite know why, and suddenly it struck me that it was because we had our feet on Danish soil again. Madsen said, "You can imagine what the feeling is on a Danish ship that has been in port for more than half a year when it finally hits the Skagen again."

We've been gorging ourselves on pastry, fruits, etc. I wrote to Hanne and started to tell her about the presents I had bought her, but then I changed my mind. I want to be there to see the look of pleasure and surprise in her eyes.

RESISTANCE AND PRISON 6

TOWARD THE END *of September Kim left the ship to work in the resistance movement.*

17 October 1944

How I long for a dash of cold salt water in my face and the sound of sails flapping in the wind, a bicycle ride on a black night, and to arrive at my destination and see a light shining from the top-floor window at Loendal! Now it's always: "Come over right away." "Can't you do this?" "That has to be done right away," etc. It's an exhausting and difficult job, but I wouldn't change it for anything.

VEDBAEK
19 October 1944

While I've been reading Lin Yutang's book, I've come to realize that there is a basic lack in our western civilization, an ancient culture which belongs to the Chinese. You feel that this culture is part of Lin Yutang, and that the Chinese have a depth and value as human beings where we amount to practically nothing.

My thoughts continue to wander along in this direction. Would I feel myself more worthy if I had all these ties with the past? Wouldn't they, however desirable, be an obstacle in the path of my freedom? In a flash I realize that I myself can acquire roots which will grow in my heart. Then, no matter what, I will be free to follow the dictates of my heart without the slightest hesitation when it urges me to do something.

HELLERUP
28 November 1944

Dear Nitte,

You must forgive me for having neglected you for so long, but I know you understand that my present life takes all of my time and that my thoughts are filled with everything that comes my way in these crucial days.

This is an extraordinary time we're living in, and it has brought forth many extraordinary people. It's almost beyond my grasp. But I do know that there is no other time in which I would prefer to have lived than the one we are now going through. Everything is trembling and the agony which is part of every birth is everywhere. Never has the world been exposed to such suffering, but never has the feeling of life been as strong or as intense as now. I'm living a fantastic life among fantastic people, and it is through this that I have come close to them. And because true feelings are always exposed when nerves are on edge, I'm getting to know people in a different way than I ever did before.

I used to look at the world through the eyes of a dreamer, and to me it's always had a special glow. Every night I went to sleep with a smile on my lips and a smile in my heart, and every morning I woke up rested and filled with wonder at the life to which I was born.

Now at night I fall into a heavy sleep, taking with me all that is on my mind. But when I wake up, it isn't because I can't sleep any longer, but because something tells me that I have work to do. It is only the present that counts. I feel that I must always follow my inner convictions, always be prepared for the unexpected, always be ready to spring into action. You know what this is like, living for the moment only and with our lives at stake. The group with which I'm working has completely accepted this.

HELLERUP
3 December 1944

Dear Nitte,

I think that I will go through a big change when I can withdraw from people and be myself again. I can't explain why or how, but I feel as if I've lost something among people that I could see, understand and feel when I was alone.

The more I live among city people, the more I realize the tremendously important role that the peace and the stillness of nature play in our development. Something is lost when you live too much among other people, the way you do in a city. The ideas and thoughts of others penetrate you, and you get so caught up in them that you are no longer able to feel or understand what is taking place in your own life.

I resent all these things that intrude themselves on me against my will. No matter how much I try to raise my head above them, I'm about to go down and will lose the ability to see things clearly which I had at sea.

Lately I've made a good friend. When it comes to money matters he's completely unreliable. This almost seems to be a matter of principle with him. He never sticks to an agreement even if it was made with the most solemn promises, and often pulls a fast one on his best friend. In spite of this he's basically absolutely honest. I work a lot with him and have gotten to like him very much. His reactions are quick as lightning and his impulses always turn out to be right. At work he is hard as nails and his manner rough, and this at first made a disagreeable impression on me, but deep down he is only a mixed-up fellow caught in the whirlpool in which we all live.

Lots of important things have happened to me since I last wrote to you. Two of my friends have disappeared, so the rest of us are pretty worried.

ON DECEMBER 19, 1944 *Kim was caught in an apartment on Classen Street, together with two friends. He was unarmed and carrying his own identification papers.*

Two days later the first letter from Kim arrived, accompanied by a familiar form letter.

> Persons who are inmates of the Vestre Prison, German Police Section, may only send and receive one letter consisting of twenty lines every two weeks. All letters must contain the prisoner's full name and birth date and must be legible. A visitor's permit may be obtained fourteen days from the date of arrest and should be addressed to the Danish Red Cross, Amaliegade 18, Copenhagen. Only one visit per month is permitted, and only one visitor is allowed. A direct appeal to the Police will be useless.
>
> Parcels containing clothing and toilet articles can be left at the prison every other Thursday between 12 and 7. No special permission is required, but it must be done in alphabetical order as follows: Thursday 12/7/44 from A-K and Thursday 12/14/44 from L-O, etc. The parcels may not contain letters or food. Tobacco and reading material may not be added without written authorization.
>
> Severe measures will be taken against anyone violating these rules. Address: German Police Section, Vestre Prison, Copenhagen V.

VESTRE PRISON,
GERMAN SECTION, CELL 252
21 December 1944

Dearest Mother,

Everything is just fine, and I'm getting adjusted to my new life much better than I had expected. This is certainly a great change, with entirely new impressions, but there is undoubtedly a lot to be learned from it all. Many times during the past two days I've thought of how wonderful it was to live at home with you and enjoy all the things that home has to give. I've also been hoping that you are feeling as calm and confident as I am. There are so many things which you can see and understand only after being separated from others. I share this cell with five other fellows, and we have lively discussions about everything under the sun. I've received permission to read and smoke, so I'd be very grateful if you would send me some tobacco and reading matter. Please don't worry. I'll be back home again before long.

I wish you all a Merry Christmas and a very Happy New Year. Please don't let the thought of me spoil your holidays. I assure you that the most difficult thing for me are my worries about you.

Thanks for the package and your greetings.

VESTRE PRISON,
GERMAN SECTION, CELL 252
10 January 1945

Dearest Nitte,

Another page has been turned, and again I see the world and people from a completely new angle. I'm sure that you're taking this in the right spirit, and that you have thought about how I would react and have put yourself in my place. To adapt myself to the life of a prisoner, and to experience his reactions, has been very interesting for me. I've often tried to imagine how I would feel at losing my freedom, and have come to the conclusion that it wouldn't be too hard to take because I would have enough to think about to keep me busy. Then I rejected this idea as blasphemous; I was like people who make a statement and then touch wood. I have gotten a great deal out of my stay here, and seldom does a day draw to a close without my being surprised that it's already over. I assure you that I felt much more confined during the time I was at school. Now I have all the time I could possibly wish for both to read and think. The conditions under which I live remind me very much of the ones I've been used to for some time, and the monotony of it leaves so much room for thought that I wouldn't have missed it for the world. I've never sidestepped an experience which came my way, and don't ever intend to. It surprises me that I don't miss my freedom more than I do, and I feel that I will probably notice how much I missed it only after I have it back again.

Again Hanne has been put through a severe test, and again our relationship has come through with increased mutual strength and confidence. I had a New Year's greeting from Mother, Ruth and Hanne. Mother and Ruth wrote how much they missed me, but Hanne wrote: "I'm the only one who doesn't miss you." Do you understand?

Remember me to the others.

VESTRE PRISON
13 January 1945

Dear ——[1]

As I have the feeling that we will probably be sent south very soon, I'm sending you this message. A hundred and sixty-five left last night.

To begin with, I want as many of you as possible to profit from the experiences I've had since my arrest. I wish that all the clandestine newspapers would publish an urgent appeal to everyone who is working for our country. We don't want to hear anything more about the gruesome methods of the Gestapo and about the unfortunate people who fall into their hands. All this should be kept off the front pages even if the

[1] This letter, written on toilet paper and smuggled out, was meant to be an appeal to Kim's friends to be published in the clandestine newspaper.

victims happen to be ministers of the gospel. We should print instead all that will serve our best interests, and only this should be put before us in print during the long job that lies ahead.

Many of us do a fine job as long as we ourselves can set the pace, but we fail when we are under duress. Let me give an example. When I was in the toilet the other day a young kid came running in like a scared rabbit, because he was about to undergo questioning. "Will they torture me in there?" He was white as a sheet. "Take it easy and don't betray your friends; nothing is going to happen to you," I said, trying to calm him down. During the questioning he immediately admitted everything and not until later did I realize that I, as well as many others who have been doing a lot of careless thinking and writing, were at fault. I should have talked to him as a man and told him that he would most likely get all hell beaten out of him, but that it wouldn't be too bad if he didn't let himself go to pieces over something so unimportant.

Everyone goes around picturing these horrors, but no one thinks that it might happen to him, just as no one thinking of death believes that he can also be touched by it himself.

The Gestapo is made up of a group of very simple men who have acquired a talent for intimidating and frightening people who are weak. But observe them more closely during the questioning. They can't disguise how uncomfortable they are and it seems as if they need all their self-control not to shoot you down on the spot because you don't tell them what they want to know. They let you understand that it is only by their kindness that you are spared. But look at the expression in their eyes, and you will see there the immense satisfaction they feel in having been able to squeeze so much out of their victim. The victim doesn't realize until later that he has been duped, and he says to himself, "If I had to go through this again, I could do a much better job of defending myself."

No one should feel that the fight is over the minute he has fallen into the hands of the enemy. That is only the beginning of the struggle to safeguard everything that others as well as you have won by fighting hard. That is the time to show whether you're a man or a coward.

I have been thinking a lot about ——. Many regard him as a hero or a martyr, but to me he was a man too weak to take part in this fight.

Please remember this. If one day you find yourself in the hands of the traitors or the Germans, brace yourself and look them straight in the eyes. The only difference is that they are now the masters over you physically. Otherwise they are the same low breed of life they were before your arrest. Take a good look at them, and you will see that the only harm they can do you is to give you some blue spots and sore muscles. Face the danger squarely today so that you will be able to take part in the proceedings of the fifth floor of the Shell Building as if they were the most normal thing in the world.

You enter a room or a corridor and are told to stand with your face against a wall. Don't stand there in a panic thinking about death. If you're afraid to die, it means that you aren't old enough to take part in the struggle for freedom, or at least not mature enough. If the thought of brute force is enough to frighten you, you are the ideal victim for questioning. Suddenly and without reason they slap you. If you're weak, the physical blow, plus the humiliation of it, will give you such a shock that the Gestapo will immediately gain the upper hand and inoculate you with so much fear that everything will move according to their wishes.

Be calm and show neither hatred nor contempt, since both of these strike out at their easily wounded vanity. Regard them as human beings and make use of this vanity to strike back at them—but very cautiously. It's amazing how easily they fall into the trap.

To bring up another point: it's sickening to see with what little trouble the Germans transport the Danes to Germany as well as to the Shell Building. We ought to take much more effective measures against their cars and equipment than we have done thus far.

Still one more thing: the Danes must change their attitude toward the Gestapo. Remember that you belong to a select group while they for the most part are a mob gone wild and therefore without scruples. Remember that this isn't a game and that you can't wave a white flag in the middle of it. This is important for the sake of our country as well as for us personally. It isn't enough to remember it; it must be instilled in your mind until it is a part of your thinking.

VESTRE PRISON
January 1945
[*smuggled out*]

Dearest Mother,

You ask if I want anything. There is only one thing: to get out of here. Otherwise I don't need anything. You know that I've always been able to get along on very little.

Thank you for what you said in your letter. It's meant a great deal to me. Your calmness and your wisdom make me very happy. You say that I've fulfilled all your expectations. I'm afraid that all of you see me in some sort of rosy light and forget to look at the facts. You forget that my daily life has prepared me for hardships much worse than the ones I've been exposed to here. Therefore you must realize that none of all the things that are so tough on the others—the food, the bed, the confinement, the questioning, have affected me in the least. I wouldn't have missed this experience for anything. Don't forget either that adventure is in my blood, and at the time of my arrest I was more excited at the thought of the experiences that were ahead of me than anything else. Neither the Gestapo nor anyone else has frightened me in the least. It's the primitive ones who are the most interesting. When they took me to the Shell Building for questioning I thought that I felt the way an animal trainer must feel when he enters a cage of wild animals. The trainer probably has a sort of affection for the animals, even if he knows that some of them are mangy and have to be destroyed. I've never been afraid of dogs, although I know that you have to proceed with caution when dealing with wild ones.

Until now I haven't been harmed. I had to take my clothes off, but that was all. The man standing beside me looked as if he were about to spring on me, but each time I ignored him without being directly impolite and started to talk to his colleague. Only once did we confront each other, and I realized what would happen if he lost control of himself. I calmly asked him, "Are you afraid?" Never have I seen a more astounded look on anyone's face. Then he flew into a rage but had to check himself because I had turned toward the other fellow, who was apparently his superior. After that he didn't flare up quite so much and did his job with a little less zest.

They asked me if I had taken a Danish customs boat to Sweden. I pretended that I hadn't understood their question, and answered that I had been to Sweden many times. They picked up their ears at this, but they weren't letting on. I made use of this opportunity to tell them that I had been to Sweden as recently as September with a schooner. At the word schooner they both looked up, and I added by way of explanation that I was a seaman. I could see them making a mental note of this.

I tried to hand them my seaman's credentials, but they weren't interested. They claimed that they already had all the necessary information. Surprised, I asked, "Did you know about me?" Yes, they knew everything. This was just fine. Without saying anything definite, I had put across the idea that it was only a short time before that I had signed off the ship. They seemed to swallow that. Then they kept on insisting that Joergen had told them that I and a fellow by the name of Knud had taken the customs ship to Sweden. I appeared very much interested and said that I had been to Nynaeshamn with the schooner. This seemed to convince them that I didn't have anything to do with the Danish customs ship, because up to now they haven't mentioned it.

Next they produced my keys. There were quite a few, since I'd also carried all of Joergen's. But I didn't want them to know that they were his. There were two key chains, and when they put them in front of me I managed to look as though they were of no particular interest. Calmly I went through the first bunch, but when they brought the second one I looked startled and said that they didn't belong to me. They asked me to whom they did belong, but of course I didn't have any idea. That was a lie, they insisted, because the keys had been found on me. I pretended to be completely taken aback. I insisted that I had never seen those keys before. I didn't look at the man to whom I had surrendered them, but I could sense that he felt less sure of himself. They looked from me to him. He hesitated, shrugged his shoulders, and since then I've heard nothing further about the keys. The questioning continued along this line until late that night. I was the only one of the three of us who was questioned so extensively. They dug up all sorts of things. Some I did know something about, but calmly denied them; in other cases it wasn't easy but I got by.

I learned fast never to say no or answer a question in the

negative because it gives them the chance to fly at you and scream that you're a liar, etc. But if you answer their questions in the affirmative, even with the most ridiculous nonsense, they often think that you've misunderstood the question, that you really don't know anything about it and let it drop.

I was a bit annoyed at the way in which you thought I had handled the situation. Take Joergen for instance—he denies everything. If only I had done the same thing. They got three things out of me. I should never have admitted that we met at my place. I should have denied knowing that Joergen was the group leader, and I should have said that I let him use the apartment once, not realizing that it would be used for a clandestine meeting. Then I would have been free today. Well, perhaps my being here will serve some purpose. I feel that it has perhaps given me the chance to accomplish more than I did before.

To get back to the point I wanted to make: you say that I have fulfilled your expectations. Now, Mother dear, don't let yourself be carried away by self-praise, because now I realize more than ever from whom I have inherited my love of adventure or rather of life itself, and I know you don't feel that this merits any praise. We live this way because we couldn't live any other way, and because it makes us happy. Basically we're egoists who follow the dictates of our own hearts. If we happen to do the right thing, we can't accept any credit for it.

P.S. you seem to think that I'm living through things which are out of the ordinary, but that's not true. It's only like going from one room to another and finding it furnished differently. And why feel sorry for a man because he is in another room!

You say that I still have a long way to go before I get there. I have no idea what you mean by "get there." I've often heard the questions asked: "What do you want to be?" "What will he do?" "What social position will he attain?" I don't know the answer to any of these. Vagabond, adventurer—something along these lines would be the only thing for me. I've often thought that I'd like to become a writer, but I'm much too restless and probably will be for many years to come. I'm the no-good son who has no particular aim in life and who doesn't do anything which doesn't happen to interest him at the moment. Most people probably pity Hanne, but I think she is ready to accept the worst.

VESTRE PRISON
[*smuggled out*]

Dear Nitte,

It was wonderful to hear from you, and this seemed to confirm the bond that exists between us. I feel so close to you, and it made me so happy to know that you feel the same way. I want to try to think about it, try to feel and understand what it is which fills us both, I in my cell and you at Loendal. But in our relationship, it's your life that has been affected—not so much mine. I have you in Loendal, Hanne at her studies, Mother in her office, while you have lost me behind a fog of conjectures—prison, cell, confinement, questioning—behind a lot of barriers which it seems impossible to penetrate, and which make it so hard for your imagination to follow me in my thoughts and feelings and to see what my life is like. But I haven't changed at all and could just as well be sitting beside you at Loendal at this moment. It's strange that you never felt too far away from me when I was in Finland or some other far-off place, but that you do now when only a locked door separates us.

Nothing happens. I'm sitting here behind four falls and a locked door and nothing happens. I keep on saying that I live in the present and I do, but in the same way as the winter crops do. They sleep peacefully under their protective covering of warm earth, waiting for the warm summer which must come before an abundant harvest can be reaped. Behind these four solid walls a wonderful feeling of peace has come over me. Nothing can happen here, in any case nothing too surprising, and that gives me a sense of drowsiness in my hibernation.

I've been doing some reading in the Bible—the New Testament. It's interesting reading and I find that I can become very much engrossed in it, but I'm somehow unable to feel myself in complete accord with it. It is as if I can't quite be stirred out of my winter sleep. Besides, the Bible isn't a book that you can pick up and read like a story. Each verse contains enough material for a full-length novel. When time lags and I feel restless and don't quite know what to do with myself, when I can't seem to concentrate on reading, I suddenly find myself writing. It's a new big discovery for me, and each time I'm amazed at the sense of freedom it gives me.

I don't understand the New Testament. I only seem to be able to see Jesus in a very few places, but perhaps I will gradually get to know the evangelists so that I can overlook their "I am better than you." When I become better acquainted with them and get to understand them and when they no longer take me by surprise, perhaps I'll be able to see something of Jesus himself, and then some of his gospel may have a deeper meaning for me.

VESTRE PRISON
21 January 1945
[*smuggled out*]

Dearest Hanne,

I've just been lying here and thinking about what a marvelous girl you really are. There are so many things in you that

I appreciate and love when I've been separated from you for a while. You're so delightfully unconcerned about all the things which occupy most people. I can't help thinking about how wonderful you were at the time of my arrest. I think you were completely calm inside.

A lot of things have happened to me while I've been here which don't happen to everybody. Don't be angry with me, but if I don't manage to get out of here I would like to be sent to Germany, first to Froeslev[1] to get to know the life there, and then to Germany to see the collapse of the Reich inside its borders. It's going to be enormously interesting. Have faith in me. I don't think that there are many as well-equipped to get through it as I am.

I've always felt that there is a reason for everything and that this chain of events is leading me some place. I feel this more strongly now than ever before. I'd feel cheated if I didn't get out of here either to see the end of the occupation and the people wild with joy here at home or else see the tragedy and breakdown in Germany.

I'm not quite sure how you stand on this, but I think you feel as I do that our lives follow lines which are not accidental and that what happens to us is always for our greatest good.

One change has taken place in me since I've been here. Before I always had a strong desire to criticize you, to change you so that you would be on the same wave length as I happened to be. I don't feel this way at all any more, and my sense of peace and confidence in our relationship is stronger than before. You radiate so much calm and light that I don't even miss you, but I wouldn't be without you for anything in the world. I wouldn't be myself any longer if I didn't have you.

I'd give a lot to know if I'm leaving for Froeslev tonight or if it isn't a false alarm as so often before. In any case I should

[1] Concentration camp in Denmark

think that I would be leaving here soon, since my case is closed.

I must say that up to the present time I've been very lucky to have the chance to live a life so full of change and movement with so many new impressions. It's really wonderful to be alive. I still don't know what death is like, but it would seem to me that it's the high point of our lives. I can't help thinking of this when I see how nervous the Gestapo and the collaborators are when they go into town. But I'm a bit different from them just the same.

22 January 1945

Here I am again, my dear little love. There was so much I wanted to tell you yesterday, but which I couldn't get down on paper, somehow. I keep on writing to you all the time, not because it brings me closer to you than I already am but being able to pour out my thoughts to you on paper is such a comfort to me.

These last few days I've been thinking a lot of present-day pharisees and the reasons why the Bible has been so thoroughly misinterpreted, and I understand how this has happened. When I read the Bible—I'm talking about the New Testament—I suddenly see Jesus clearly behind a few lines of text only to have him disappear again behind a flow of words from the evangelists. Slowly the weight of them wears me down, and since we are all slaves of words we are dulled by them and submerged in them until they become a part of our life.

Today I was standing on the bench and looking out of the window, and suddenly my thoughts of the other day were right there before me in exactly the same way as the landscape below. The last time I saw it, all was gray and dismal with nothing special to catch the eye, and today it is all dressed in glittering white with the frosty winter sky arching over it. In a flash I saw my thoughts of yesterday in a new light. The teachings of Jesus shouldn't be followed like a lesson learned by heart and interpreted literally. We shouldn't live by his commandments but according to them, and this should come from the depths of our hearts like every real inspiration and not from the outside.

The most important thing that Jesus has taught me is that we should be governed only by our most profound convictions. You probably feel that this goes without saying, and of course you're right. I've always felt this way, but I never fully realized before all the truth that is concentrated in these words. I can't help thinking of Jesus when he makes the peddlers leave the temple. It seems that at that moment he was filled with fury and indignation. But man's mind has many facets, and love and hate aren't very far removed.

Dearest, I've so often wished that you would feel the strength and the joy which come with inspiration, and wondered how I could have you share this experience with me. I don't mean romantic or poetic daydreams; I'm thinking of the experience it is to look into your own heart and to discover that what is there is no illusion but a reality.

Thanks for your letter which was just handed to me. You can't imagine what it means to me every time I hear from all of you outside. I hope you understand that when I say something, it isn't in order to criticize you. It's only that I want to help you and I want you to feel that you and I belong together to such a degree that criticism doesn't exist between us but only a desire to aim higher. Can't you be like a foal out in the pasture for the first time? When you see the foal, you're happy because you know that your life can be as free as his. Then all of a sudden you sense that you're not alone, that someone is watching you. It's me standing by the gate. My little darling, can't you see that I love the foal most when it kicks, although I may try to calm it down. Its mere presence, untamed, right next to me makes me so incredibly happy. It doesn't pay any attention to what I say, but goes galloping off happy to be alive. I know that you can't completely let yourself be carried away by spring as long as I'm standing down there at the gate calmly watching you. But you know, I'm a foal too and it's not in order to watch you that I'm standing by the gate. The air is too heavy with spring, and there is too much stirring in me. It's when I seem to be the most annoying onlooker that I feel freer and more full of life than you've ever been. I am with you with all my heart, dancing with you through the fields in a jubilant spring mood. I long for you so terribly, your physical presence, to feel your warmth, and more than that, to have a piece of your heart here with me so that mine can merge with yours in leaps of joy. Be the foal who rears without reason, who joyfully frisks about so full of life that he can hardly bear it.

I want to feel that you have been on a visit in my heart, wandered all around in it and that you have accepted and understood everything there. You say that you'll never really understand me, but what does that matter as long as you and I can play as foals together on a green meadow on a morning in spring.

ON FEBRUARY 5 *Kim was sent to the camp at Froeslev together with some other prisoners. In the meantime the Gestapo had obtained new evidence against him. Upon his arrival at Froeslev his name was called out and he was placed in solitary confinement. Three or four days later he was sent back to Vestre Prison.*

When they were clearing out the prison after the German capitulation, one of the resistance fighters found a letter which Kim had received from Nitte toward the end of February. On the back of this letter he wrote the following, probably to give vent to his feelings, never thinking that it would ever be read. The entire sheet was covered with microscopic writing, possibly continued elsewhere or was to be continued, because "as you" was squeezed in the lower right-hand corner of the page. At any rate, the rest has never been found. From witnesses inside the prison we know that Kim was brought back to the cell unconscious, after having been tortured.

3 March 1945

Yesterday I was sitting at the table. I looked at my hands in amazement. They were trembling. I thought about it for a moment. There are some things which produce a purely physical reaction. Suddenly, as I was sitting here, I was possessed by the desire to draw something. I got up and started to sketch on the wall. I was fascinated and became more and more absorbed. Under my hand suddenly appeared a farmer, standing by a barbed-wire fence. I sat down, got up and made some changes, sat down again and felt much better. This was much better than anything I'd ever done before. All day I worked on it. There were so many things which I couldn't make come out the way I wanted them to. I studied it, stretched my imagination to the utmost and was suddenly completely exhausted. I erased all of it and since then even the idea of drawing makes me sick.

I've been thinking about this strange experience a good deal. Right afterwards I had such a wonderful feeling of relief, a sense of having won a victory and such intense happiness that I felt quite numb. It seemed as if body and soul became separated, one in a wild and soaring freedom beyond the reach of the world, and the other doubled up in a horrible cramp which held it to the earth. I suddenly realized how terrifically strong I am (but perhaps I only tried to talk myself into this). When the body and soul rejoined forces, it was as if all the joys of the world were right there for me. But it was as with so many stimulants; when the effect wore off the reaction set in. I saw that my hands were shaking, something had given inside. It was as if there had been a short circuit in the roots of my heart which drained it of all strength. I was like a man hungry for pleasure and consumed by desire. But still I was calm and in better spirits than ever before.

Although I feel no fear, my heart beats faster every time someone stops outside my door. It's a physical reaction although it's caused by a sensory perception.

Right afterwards I realized that now I understood something else about Jesus. It's the period of waiting that is the real test. I'm sure that to have a few nails driven through one's hands and to die on a cross is only a physical ordeal; the spirit is in a state of elation which can't be compared with anything else. But the period of waiting in the garden causes red blood to flow.

Strange, but I didn't feel any resentment or hatred at all. Something happened to my body, which is only the body of an adolescent, and it reacted as such, but my mind was elsewhere. It was aware of the small creatures who were busying themselves with my body, but it was in a world of its own and too engrossed to pay much attention to them.

I've learned something by being alone. It is as if I'd reached rock bottom in myself, which usually can't be seen for all the layers of egotism, conceit, love, and all the ups and downs of daily life. It is this which makes me feel as if I'd had a short cricuit within me. When I'm with other people, their interests, their conversation, act as a balm, covering the rock bottom in myself with a warm compress. When I'm alone, it is as if layers of skin were being scraped away. Your mind is not at ease, you can't concentrate on reading, the spirit as well as the body must keep on pacing up and down. I suddenly understood what insanity must be, but I knew that this was like everything else which has happened to me, and in a couple of days I'll be myself again.

Sometimes a beautiful scene flashes before my eyes, but none of you are in it. I see myself riding on horseback out in the fields. But I must have children around me, not adults. I've been longing for the sea, but it has to be calm, because I couldn't stand being seasick at the moment. It was funny seeing that horse; it brought my whole childhood back again.

21 March 1945

My dearest little love,[1]

On Wednesday, February 21st, at midnight I was sent to Police Headquarters for questioning, and on Wednesday, the 28th, I was sent back to Vestre. On Thursday I was placed in solitary confinement and forbidden to write letters. I was only allowed to go to the toilet morning and night with a guard when there was no one in the corridors. My food was brought by the soldiers. I was happy to be alone in my cell. I took off all my clothes and had a good wash and it gave me such a sense of freedom. That night I slept in a bed with sheets and a mattress.

I did some thinking and meditating, and the days passed very pleasantly. I had opened my window, and the sun was shining. I could smell spring in the air, the grass shooting out of the ground, the moist earth. I could hear the birds singing, and such a big streak of sunshine came in through the bars that I could sit on the bench and let it warm my face.

[1] Pasted on the inside of a Red Cross carton and found after Kim's death

On Monday, March 5, I was transferred to Police Headquarters and put in Detention. On Wednesday they allowed me to receive my blanket.

Have been in the following cells: December 19, 1944 to February 2, 1945, in 252; from the same day at 8 o'clock, in 585 (dark cell); February 7 to 11, Froeslev. From February 12 to March 1 occupied the following cells in Vestre: 286, 284, 282, 276, 270. From March 1 to 5 in 586. Was then transferred to Police Headquarters: March 5 to 12, cell 50, March 12 to —? cell 37.

Twice I've been waiting in the cells of the Shell Building to be questioned so I think that I've been living a rather varied cell life. The cell I had when I sat in Detention was on the small side—6 feet, 3 inches by 4 feet—with a small bench and a table. I walked up and down—one and a half paces in each direction; twenty-four hours and all alike, only broken by the opening of the door when two slices of rye bread were handed to me. This was a real event. In the toilet they allowed me to wash, and it was wonderful. Then I paced up and down again, very much surprised that I didn't suffer. I thought of the days spent in solitary confinement and how rewarding they had been. I had the sun, the blue sky, and once in a while a little white cloud, and if I really made an effort I could see a plowed field, grass, people, and lots of other fascinating things. I could smell the earth and feel the coming of spring. It made me choke up inside and I felt very happy. All this had such a sound and soothing effect on my mind.

They say that the Shell Building was bombed yesterday and this upset me very much. Your school is so close by. Something could have happened to you, you might even have been killed, and here I sit writing to you not knowing if you're alive or if you will ever read this. How will I be able to find out how you are! But there are so many possibilities—perhaps you weren't even there yesterday.

We have been talking about what is really meant by art. I know what it means to me, but how could I possibly put it into words. Isn't an artist a person who can produce riches from the depths of himself and put them before people so that their lives will in turn be enriched by his art? But the minds of people must be prepared and fertilized in order to be able to accept it. One has to be a part of this era, be inspired by it, and in turn freely give of oneself to it. Only then can the untapped sources of man be reached—the forces that constitute a true artist.

Jesus lives among us, but he is much older and much more mature than the Jesus who lived at the time of the Apostles. He is like every other human being who has lived and grown spiritually, and I'm deeply convinced that he went through what every artist does—in fact, every human being. When I meet an old man, I can see in him the truth around which his life was formed, and which was awakened with his birth.

Jesus has grown older, and many people ask themselves if he ever really lived and if he wasn't simply the culmination of the Hebrew doctrine. I think I know what they mean but can't help asking myself, "This old man, has he ever been a child?"

I've caught lice, but I hope that I've gotten rid of them again. I had an awful lot of bites, and the itching almost drove me mad. Today I examined my clothes, which haven't been off my back for three weeks since I sleep on the floor with only a blanket over me. There were masses of eggs and lice. But now I've washed myself and my clothes so I hope this is the end of it.

I'm kept going by one thought: that nothing is impossible no matter how black things look at the moment. There are millions of possibilities which can't be foreseen, and no situation exists which can't be completely changed in a moment.

I'm lying on a mattress on the floor and letting the sun shine on my face. There are five of us in the cell. One of them is pacing up and down. Every time he comes toward me, his shadow falls on my face and again when he walks back. It is as if a switch was turned on and off inside me at regular intervals; like a little current of irritation which goes through me but completely vanishes when the sun touches my face again.

Today is Sunday and the weather is still perfect. How I would love to go for a walk in the woods with you, my darling! The sun has been shining since early morning and I've been lying here by the window watching the rays of light come through the blackout curtain and spreading out more and more. The air full of spring and morning came streaming down to me. A migration of birds flew over the rooftops and they must have been huge ones to judge by the flapping of their wings. This sound made something stir in me, and all of a sudden I felt so lighthearted. It was as if this migration held out a special promise for me, like spring itself, which is always full of promise of something new and fascinating for each of us. I didn't feel at all the way tame ducks do when their free brothers pass by up in the sky. My existence is much too quiet and peaceful for me to envy them, but I do know that the moment when I stand under a blue sky again my happiness will be without bounds.

As I was lying here happy that spring is here and that you and I are alive (I know now that you're safe and that nothing has happened to you), I was thinking about what this spring might have in store for us—certainly things far different from what we had imagined. Still, it may possibly be one of the happiest of our lives.

27 March 1945

I've been smoking some, and have noticed that it has a soothing effect when the nerves are on edge, but that the reaction is exactly the opposite when I'm calm. I don't think that I would ever smoke when I'm free. It makes me jittery, and seems to leave the mind empty. It is as if tobacco takes something out of you and leaves you feeling like a vacuum. I'm annoyed in the same way I am when I feel that I'm not making any progress.

I've often thought of the speech that Socrates made in his own defense, and also of the last time I was brought in for questioning. Socrates says in his introduction that he knows in advance what the outcome will be and that he will not be able, during the few hours at his disposal, to overcome the resentment they feel against him, a resentment which has worked into them like so many small, fine needle pricks during the years, so that it is now part of them. He knows that it would take a long time to erase an image and create a new one. I felt the same way. For many years the people I had to deal with had been taught to see things in a certain light and their minds were set against me. My hands were tied in every way so my only means of expressing myself was by the answers I had to give to the questions they asked. I know what Socrates must have gone through and I understand that a man as wise as he couldn't have acted in any other way.

Jesus has also been in my mind a lot of late. I can understand his boundless love for all humanity, and especially for those who put the nails through his hands. The moment he left Gethsemane he rose above every human passion. It was only during the period of waiting that he felt fear, the way Kaj Munk must have felt before he was taken out to the car, and before he came in contact with those who were to be his executioners. The moment he drove off with them he must have felt above it all, and this must have given him both dignity and strength.

The same with Jesus. At the moment when Judas kissed him on the cheek he had certainly regained all his peace of mind and his feeling of being above it all. Then he was swept up by an enormous wave which finally carried him to his death. It so filled his mind that he didn't have an instant's fear or hesitation. When he met his executioners they put him physically out of the material life. He felt so liberated, so uplifted, that he no longer saw them with the eyes of a human being, but with infinite wisdom and compassion, which creates understanding of the level on which the others find themselves.

The cleansing of the spirit makes you see the world from a new level way above what is known as pain or fear. You are already so far above the world and so immobile up there that the instinctive hatred which comes as a result of fear disappears. Those who are close to us in our lives can't reach us at a moment like this. They remain in the background, and it is only in passing that you send them a loving thought, whereas all that has been in the background of your life—your most sacred and unattainable ideals—suddenly grow into the main substance of the soul.

In a ray of light, Jesus saw for the last time his whole life pass before him. Fear comes from within, and if someone tries to produce a feeling of fear in another human being, he only succeeds in freeing him from all fear and causing him to rise to a plane where he cannot be reached.

It's Easter, and I've received a package from Nis [sic] today —it was wonderful.

Yesterday I wrote that in a moment like this you rise to a level where those who are near and dear only receive a loving thought in passing while your innermost thoughts come to the foreground and fill your being. Please don't misunderstand me, because this isn't exactly true either, but keep it in mind as you read the rest of this, and afterwards try to merge these two thoughts into one. This will perhaps bring us a little closer to the real truth.

At a moment like this, you're a big, trembling animal, alive and absolutely pure. There isn't a shadow anywhere, not a drop of hatred or fury, because these feelings couldn't germinate and grow in such an atmosphere of purity and simplicity. At that moment there isn't the slightest restraint or obstacle in your mind, and that is probably why the feeling of purity and freedom fills your being. It is as if your heart opened and a marvelous little green bud began to grow.

The moment fills you with a feeling of peace and devotion and the arch above your head seems very high. From where you are the people around you appear in an entirely different light. Do you think that a father in church, seeing his beloved holding their first-born child over the baptismal, notices the people around him? Don't you think that his heart is so overflowing with tenderness and love that he feels only affection for everything around him?

When I went up for questioning, or perhaps when I was already there, I said to myself all of a sudden, "If you could only come out in the woods with me as woodcutters, away from everything, even if only for a short time, a change would come about in you—perhaps not a permanent change because you are made of different material—but so that you would see and feel, for a little while at least, how profound life is and how rich is the world around you which you refuse to understand. This also flashed through my mind: "Have these men ever seen the reflection of the moon in a little pond in the forest, or have they ever seen the wind playing in the grass on the dunes before it drifts out over the edge and down toward the sea?"

Last night I had a long discussion with my cellmates and for the first time I felt that I would have liked to write something for the theatre, and I also know what it would have been. I could see the dark cell where the bars cast their black shadows on the wall bathed in moonlight. Four men are stretched out on the floor talking, each one with his ideals and ideas, each one with his own convictions, each with a different point of view. Suddenly I realized how much is still needed before we can consider ourselves a free people. Perhaps we'll be liberated, but will we be free? A country where every man has his personal opinion and has the courage to be responsible for it before God and man; where man isn't only an echo of the opinions and the reflection of his environment?

Just think how different Denmark could have been today.

VESTRE PRISON
GERMAN SECTION, CELL 411
4 April 1945

My own little darling,

Today I was taken before the military tribunal and condemned to death. What a terrible blow this is for a little girl of twenty! I've been given permission to write this farewell letter, but what shall I write? How shall I formulate my swan song? Time is short and there is so much to say.

What is the final and most precious thing I can give you? What do I possess that I can leave you as a parting gift so that in spite of your loss you will smile and go on living and developing?

We sailed on a stormy sea, we met in the trusting way of playing children and we loved each other. We still love each other and always will, but one day a storm separated us. I went aground while you were washed up on shore, and you are going to continue living in a new world. I don't expect you to forget me. Why should you forget something so beautiful as that which existed between us? But you mustn't become a slave to this memory. You must keep on going with the same easy and graceful approach to life as before and twice as happy because on your way Life gave you one of its greatest gifts. Free yourself—let this greatest of joys be everything to you, let it shine brighter and clearer than anything else, but let it be only one of your most treasured memories. Don't let it blind you and keep you from seeing all the wonderful things life has in store for you. Don't be unhappy, my dearest one. You must mature and grow rich in inner resources. Do you understand this, my beloved?

You will live on and you will have other beautiful adventures, but promise me—this you owe to everything I have lived for—that never will the thought of me come between you and Life. Remember, I will continue to live in your heart, but the part of me which remains there should be sound and natural and mustn't take up too much room. Gradually as bigger and more important things appear, I shall glide into the background and be a tiny speck of the soil out of which your happiness and your development will keep on growing.

Now you are heartbroken and this is what is known as sorrow, but Hanne, look beyond this. All of us are going to die and it isn't for us to judge whether my going a little earlier is good or bad.

I keep on thinking about Socrates. Read him and you will find Plato expressing what I feel at this moment. My love for you is without bounds, but not more so now than before. It's not a love which causes me pain. This is the way it is, and I want you to understand it. There is something inside me alive and growing—an inspiration, a love—call it what you like;

something which I still haven't been able to define. Now I'm going to die and I still don't know if I have started a little flame in another being, a flame which will survive me. But still, my mind is at rest because I've seen the richness and abundance of nature. No one takes notice if a few seeds are trampled under and die. When I see all the riches that still live on, why should I despair?

Lift up your head, my most precious love, and look! The sea is still blue, the sea which I loved and which has enveloped us both. Now you will live for the two of us. I am gone and what remains is not a memory which will make you into a woman like S., but mold you into a woman living and warm, mature and happy. This does not mean that you are to try to rise above sorrow, because then you will become rigid and assume a saintly attitude with regard to your faith in me and in yourself, and you will lose what I most loved in you—that you are first and last and always a woman.

Remember—and I swear this is true—that all sorrow gradually turns into happiness. But few are those who admit it when the time comes. They cloak themselves in mourning; habit makes them think that it is sorrow, and so they continue to cloak themselves in it. The truth is that after suffering comes maturity and after this maturity the fruits are gathered.

You see, Hanne, one day you will meet the man who will be your husband. The thought of me will flash through you, and you will perhaps deep down have a vague, uneasy feeling that you are betraying me or something in you which is pure and sacred. Lift up your head once more, Hanne, look straight into my eyes which are smiling at you and you will understand that the only way to betray me is by not completely following your natural instincts. When you see him, let your heart go out to meet him—not to drown your sorrow but because you truly love him. You will be very, very happy because you now have a base on which feelings still unknown to you will nurture.

Greet Nitte for me. I've thought of writing her but don't know if I'll have the time. I seem to feel as if I could do more for you because all that is life to me is now concentrated on you. I would like to breathe into you all the life that is in me, so that it can go on and as little as possible of it go to waste. This is the way I was made.

Yours, but not for always.

VESTRE PRISON
GERMAN SECTION, CELL 411
4 April 1945

Dearest Mother,

Today I went before the military tribunal together with Joergen, Niels and Ludwig. We were condemned to die. I know that you're strong and that you will be able to take this. But listen to me, Mother. It isn't enough that you are able to take it. You must also understand it. I'm not of importance and will soon be forgotten, but the ideas, the life, the inspiration which filled me will live on. You will find them everywhere—in the new green of spring, in people you will meet on your way, in a loving smile. Perhaps you will also find what was of value to me, you will love it and you won't forget me. I would have liked to grow and mature, but I will still live in your hearts and you will live on because you know that I am in front of you on the road and not behind, as you had perhaps thought at first. You know what has always been my greatest wish and what I thought I would become. Mother dear, come with me on my journey. Don't stop at the last stage of my life, but instead stop at some of the preceding ones and you may find something which will be of value to the girl I love and to you, Mother.

I have followed a certain path and I don't regret it. I've never betrayed what is in my heart, and now I seem to see the unbroken line which has run through my life. I'm not old, I ought not to die, and still, it seems so simple and natural to me. It's only the brutal way which at first terrifies us. I have so little time left; I don't quite know how to explain it, but my mind is completely at peace. I have always wanted to be like Socrates, but although I have no one to talk to as he had, I feel the same tranquility of spirit and very much want you, Hanne and Nitte to understand this. Remember me to Nitte; I love her dearly and meant every word I ever wrote.

How strange it seems to be writing this testament! Each word will stand; it can never be amended, never revoked, never changed. I'm thinking of so many things. Joergen is sitting here in front of me writing a letter to his daughter for her Confirmation—a document for life. We have lived together as friends and now we're going to die together. We have shared the same cell with Paul and we've had many differences but he knows me well by now and what I have to contribute.

Finally there are the children who have recently come to mean so much to me. I had so been looking forward to seeing them and being with them again. Just to think of them makes me happy and I hope they will grow up to be men who will be able to get more out of life than what lies on the surface. I hope that their character will develop freely and never be subjected to prejudice.

Give them my love, my godson and his brother.

I see what the situation in our country is leading up to and I know that Grandfather is right. But remember all of you that the aim shouldn't be to return to the period before the war, but that it is up to you, young and old, to create a broad, human ideal which everyone can recognize. This is the thing that our country needs; something that even a simple peasant boy can look up to and be happy in the thought that he is working and fighting for.

Then, finally, there is my Hanne. Make her see that the pilot stars are still shining and that I was only a beacon on her route. Help her to keep going. She can now become very happy.

In haste—your oldest and only son.

DOCUMENTS 7

Because of the reader's natural interest in Kim's activities as a Danish patriot, the documents relating to his sentence and execution have been included in this book.

FOREIGN OFFICE, COPENHAGEN
7 April 1945

It was with deep regret that the Foreign Office yesterday had to forward to you a communication from the High Commissioner of the German Reich stating that the request to commute the sentence of your son, Mr. Kim Malthe-Bruun, has been denied and that the death sentence was carried out yesterday morning. In order that you may know the exact terms used in the communication which the Foreign Office has received from the High Commissioner of the Reich, we are herewith sending you a copy of the message from the High Commissioner dated 6 April 1945, together with an abstract of the decree of the court.

The Foreign Office wishes to express its profound sympathy in the great loss you and your family have suffered.

(signed) F. M. Nils Svenningsen

Mrs. Vibeke Malthe-Bruun
c/o Commander M.E. Malthe-Bruun
Taarbaek Strandvej 20,
pr. Klampenborg

HIGH COMMISSIONER FOR THE
GERMAN REICH IN DENMARK
COPENHAGEN
6 April 1945

Director of the Royal Danish Ministry of Foreign Affairs
Mr. Nils Svenningsen
Copenhagen

Dear Mr. Svenningsen:

With reference to my letter of April 5, 1945 and to your

letter of the same date, I wish to inform you that the death sentences pronounced against

Count Ludvig Alfred Otto Reventlow
Joergen Frederik Winther
Kim Malthe-Bruun and
Peter Fynn

unfortunately cannot be commuted because the actions of the condemned may constitute a danger to the Wehrmacht because of the arms collected and distributed by them.

These sentences were today carried out by shooting.

I am enclosing an abstract of the verdict against the aforesaid as well as four other verdicts which rendered sentences of hard labor.

The verdict will be published on 8 April 1945.

Yours truly,

(signed) W. Best

ABSTRACT OF THE SENTENCE PASSED BY THE MILITARY TRIBUNAL OF THE GERMAN POLICE, DATED *April 4, 1945*

Danish subject, Seaman Kim Malthe-Bruun, born July 8, 1923 in Schashewan-Forts,[1] Canada, Mother's name: Vibeke Malthe-Bruun, Copenhagen, Callisenvej 25, has been condemned to death for partisan action. As a member of the illegal group Joergen Winther, he has commandeered a customs boat to Sweden. He returned to Denmark on the S.S. *Wanjan*. This ship carried illegal weapons brought back for use by the Winther group, and Malthe-Bruun took an active part in transporting these weapons from the port of Copenhagen. He was aware of the fact that these weapons were destined to combat the German armed forces. According to Paragraph 3

[1] Fort Saskatchewan

of the Special War Crimes Code, the death sentence was obligatory.

Attested:
Copenhagen 5 April 1945
(Name)
Hauptwachtmeister d. Schp.d. Res. (Master Sergeant)
(Security Police Reserve)

GUENTHER PANCKE

SS Brigade Commander and Police General
SS and Police Chief in Denmark

Ref. O.U. 4-4-45

Commander Malthe-Bruun (ret.)
Klampenborg, Taarbaek Strandvej 20

Dear Commander Malthe-Bruun:

It is to my great regret that I have to convey to you the sad news that it has been impossible for me to commute the sentence passed today against your grandson, Kim Malthe-Bruun, and the members of his group by the Special Court Marshal.

It was not possible for me to interfere with the law or the application of justice in order to commute the sentence or grant clemency since otherwise other sentences against Danish saboteurs and terrorists would have been unjust.

I have already informed your niece, Miss Anna Ida Bruun, that your grandson was accused of severe violations against martial law since he on several occasions has taken an active and leading role in actions which have greatly harmed the German armed forces in Denmark.

Since he took part in these activities together with an illegal group, he had to be tried in court and sentenced together with this group. The sentence is severe in accordance with the martial law in force, and therefore he and three other members of his group were condemned to die.

As a former soldier you will certainly understand that this action had to be taken. In a war such as the one which Germany is now compelled to fight it is the duty of all officers guarding the security of the German Reich to combat our enemies by all available means. You will understand that those who participate in military action as partisans behind the lines of the German Armed Forces, and under the protection of civilian clothes, must bear the punishment prescribed by martial law.

It is most painful for me to have to inform you and your niece of the action taken.

Yours truly,

(signed) Pancke

Communique FROM THE PRESS BUREAU OF THE SS AND POLICE CHIEF IN DENMARK

In accordance with martial law, the following Danish subjects have been condemned to death:

1. Peter Fynn, student, born 6.13.1920 in Copenhagen, residing in Copenhagen: for having procured weapons for the Danish resistance movement in his capacity of leader of an illegal organization. He has already participated in the transport of illegal weapons.

2. Kim Malthe-Bruun, seaman born 7.8.1923 in Schashewan-Forts, Canada, residing in Copenhagen, member of an illegal group, for having stolen a customs boat and having com-

mandeered it to Sweden. He has also procured weapons for his group and participated in the transport of weapons.

3. Count Ludvig Alfred Otto Reventlow, chargé d'affaires, born 2.16.1916 in Aarhus, residing in Copenhagen, for having participated in the transport of weapons and explosives for an illegal group.

4. Joergen Frederik Winther, chargé d'affaires, born 4.26.1917 in Copenhagen, where he is a resident, for having organized a transport of weapons as leader of a clandestine group.

The condemned have been shot.

Furthermore, the following persons have been condemned to hard labor:

1. Poul Martin Poulsen, foreman, born 4.25.1913 in Thoreby, residing in Copenhagen, fifteen years for aiding the enemy by hiding arms and explosives.

2. Edward Collin, senior physician, born 10.8.1886 in Copenhagen, residing at Lyngby near Copenhagen, ten years for having aided the enemy by financially supporting an illegal group.

3. Hans E. Lehrman, engineer, born 9.10.1893 in Jordloese, residing in Copenhagen, eight years for aiding the enemy by having worked in his garage for an illegal group.

4. Kurt Eberlin Christensen, manager, born 7.5.1911 in Copenhagen, residing in Copenhagen, eight years for aiding the enemy by financially supporting an illegal group.

BOSTON PUBLIC LIBRARY
3 9999 00007 072 0